REBEL HUMOR

120 Stories of the Comical Side
of Confederate Army Service, 1861-1865

Gregory A. Coco

Savas Beatie
California

Originally published separately by Thomas Publications in 1999

Library of Congress Control Number: 2022939360

First Savas Beatie Edition, First Printing

ISBN-13: 978-1-61121-652-3
eISBN: 978-1-954547-54-4 (Savas Publishing)

SB

Savas Beatie
989 Governor Drive, Suite 102
El Dorado Hills, CA 95762
916-941-6896
www.savasbeatie.com
sales@savasbeatie.com

Savas Beatie titles are available at special discounts for bulk purchases by corporations, institutions, and others. For more details, please contact contact us at sales@savasbeatie.com or visit www.savasbeatie.com for more information.

Cover illustration by Charles R. Hazard
Original illustrations by Charles R. Hazard and John Heiser

To Keri,

My first was for you,
The twelfth is too.

THE
GREGORY A. COCO
COLLECTION

by Savas Beatie

A Strange and Blighted Land: Gettysburg—The Aftermath of a Battle

On the Bloodstained Field:
Human Interest Stories of the Campaign and Battle of Gettysburg

A Vast Sea of Misery: A History and Guide to the Union and Confederate Field Hospitals
at Gettysburg, July 1-November 20, 1863

Confederates Killed in Action at Gettysburg

Wasted Valor: The Confederate Dead at Gettysburg

A Concise Guide to the Artillery at Gettysburg

Killed in Action: Eyewitness Accounts of the Last Moments
of 100 Union Soldiers Who Died at Gettysburg

Rebel Humor: 120 stories of the
Comical Side of Confederate Army service, 1861-1865

War Stories: A Collection of One Hundred Fifty Little-Known
Human Interest Stories of the Campaign and Battle of Gettysburg

The Civil War Infantryman: In Camp, on the March, and in Battle

Two Confederate Officers Remember Gettysburg:
Col. Robert M. Powell, 5th Texas Infantry, Hood's Texas Brigade
& Capt. George Hillyer, 9th Georgia Infantry

*"Did you ever think, sir,
what an opportunity a battlefield
affords liars?"*

— Gen. T.J. Jackson, 1862

Introduction

"The serious and the humorous were very closely united in the experience of soldiers," wrote Lieutenant George W. Beale of the 9th Virginia Cavalry, C.S.A. "The moments and spots filled with danger and anxiety were often filled also with amusement and laughter." Beale added the following additional observations, which are certainly pertinent to a book dealing with Confederate humor:

> It might be supposed that the soldiers of the South, who were called to stand amidst so many terrors of the battle, to contend against enormous odds, to subsist on half rations, and to go often for days without even these, and, above all, to know as so many did that their families—wives and children, aged parents and sisters—were in the enemy's lines, exposed to depredation, pillage, and insult, would wear long faces, have bowed heads, and be little given to laughter and mirth. Such, however, was not the case. Their marches were enlivened with many a joke, and their camps rang often with peals of merriment and outbursts of jovial hilarity.
>
> Perhaps, the serious side of their lives which at times became as stern as death and as solemn as the grave had a natural rebound, and the pendulum of their spirits having swung far in one direction again swung back with a greater force. It was easy for a joke to be started among them, and when once started it passed readily from one to another, so that a thousand camp-fires became the scenes of its repetition and enjoyment. Our cavalrymen had keen eyes to discover the ludicrous side of happenings, if there were any to be seen, and when one of them became a good subject of fun and laughter, their sportive mirth was soon shared by a great multitude.[1]

"[T]he Southern soldier is an inveterate *farceur*," commented Richard W. Corbin, a French speaking officer on the staff of Confederate General Charles W. Field, meaning, of course, that the average man in the ranks was a jokester and a comic of the highest degree. Corbin also described the rank and file Rebels as much akin to naughty schoolboys, who were "sadly addicted to mischief." Corbin, like most other officers, had come in contact with these "jesters" or "wags," as they were called, too often not to have felt the sting of their barbs. For the last thing a man needed was to be caught *mounted* and unknown in the midst of an infantry column, wearing either fancy footwear, a new uniform, or an unusual hat. Corbin, fresh from his home in France, sporting a beautiful English saddle and fine, tall European boots, was never able to ride through a marching regiment without becoming the particular target of some infantryman spouting homespun witticisms. "I say Mister, come out of them boots, I see your head a-peeping out," or else, "Get a Corkscrew for the gentleman, he wants to get out of his boots." But no matter what the situation, warned Corbin, you should not become hostile, arrogant, or overbearing, for then your fate was sealed. "I say, Bill, look at that there officer; he's raither stiff and stuck-up, ain't he?"

"Yes, I reckon he had ramrod tea for breakfast," etc., etc., until the unfortunate and stranded fellow begged for mercy.[2]

Captain D. Augustus Dickert of the 3rd South Carolina similarly recalled the "exuberant spirits" of the average Southern fighting man, who "yelled at everything he saw, from an ox-cart to a pretty woman, [the] downfall of a luckless cavalryman [or] a charge in battle." He noted too that war had its "humorous as well as serious side, and many a joke was cracked in battle," or if not then, soon afterwards.

Others recounted the lighter side and devilish nature of the Confederate soldier, and the fact that in every regiment there could be found, always, a few professional "comics," or "wags." A 20th Tennessean, William J. McMurray, claimed his unit had a fellow so famous for his antics that even the enemy got to know him personally. He was Dave Montgomery; six foot, four inches tall, beardless and "gangling," and his fame spread far and wide. McMurry said Dave was "chuck full of wit and would always press himself forward to 'sass' someone." The "life" of the regiment, Montgomery took great delight in cursing and abusing the Yankees out on the skirmish line. When in close quarters, the boys in blue would holler out, "where is Dave Montgomery? lookout Dave."

"Our soldier boys are as full of mischief as a cat is of fleas," is how William Andrews, a Georgia sergeant, described the merriment of some of his regiment. He added the acknowledgment that, "[t]he boys are going to have their fun, and the best you can do is to take it like a little man, because if you get mad and want to fight, you will certainly be accommodated. The boys mean no harm, and if it was not for the mischief carried on in camps, all would die of the blues." Andrews complimented several of the boys in his 1st Georgia Regulars who constantly engaged in fun and pranks. They "never get tired or in the blues," noted the sergeant. "When the rest are completely tired out, they are ready for a frolic."[3]

Another Confederate, an articulate officer named Robert Stiles, felt that there was "a spirit of lighthearted jollity and fun" which characterized the men of his old battery, the Richmond Howitzers. His brother William Stiles told him that until the deadly struggles of the 1864 campaign in Virginia began, the men of the Howitzers, who were former schoolmates and friends and neighbors, were imbued with a "bounding, buoyant spirit," full of "effervescent outbursts." The "quips, the jests, the jokes, [and] the jollities," declared William, became a trademark of his artillerymen comrades.[4]

Alabama infantryman William F. Fulton, in his memoir, remarked that even under trying conditions his companions could always regain their spirits. Laughter and joking helped difficult trials to be forgotten, and as long as the "jibes flew thick and fast," serious times could be turned into a game. "This is characteristic of the southern soldier," said Fulton. "He is always in a good humor and can find fun in the hardest luck and this helps to bear him up. Even on the battlefield he is sure to see the funny side of things."[5]

Tiring marches were often enlivened by the humorist in the ranks, reported North Carolina Major W.A. Smith of the 14th Regiment. According to Smith, humor allowed the men to temporarily forget their fatigue and the harsh environment they occupied. Friendly "sallies" toward mounted couriers, officers, and civilians along the roadside, "aroused good comradeship and provoked the laughter of the tired boys." Smith believed it was usually the work of but a few of the men in his regiment who *started* the fun; however, the rest of the members were not far behind in joining in. It was *that*, he remembered, "which made our privations tolerable, [and] kept us from freezing and starvation."[6]

One of General J.E.B. Stuart's staff officers probably put it best when he declared:

> *War develops an infinite amount of wit and humor among soldiers. In every company there were aspirants for the honor of being the "funny man" of the command, whose study it was to get off good jokes; and between the companies of a regiment there was rivalry as to whose man should produce the best and make a regimental reputation. Every conceivable subject on the line of march was made to contribute to this harmless amusement and the officers encouraged it, submitting good-humoredly to being sometimes the victims themselves. The clatter of tongues and merry laughter along a dusty road would make one think they belonged to the [female] sex, bless their dear talkative hearts.[7]*

Lieutenant Albert T. Goodloe, 35th Alabama, vividly recollected many interesting situations during his army service. But he revealed that no matter how "tight" or uncomfortable these were, some soldier always came up with a humorous remark:

> *In the dreariest of bivouacs, under the sorest of privations, on the hardest of marches, and even in the lulls of battle, the ludicrous would pop out of some one, not necessarily a wag, and often to the unspeakable relief of his comrades who were enduring next to intolerable tension. Blessings upon the head of the old Reb who could give us something to laugh at when our agonies would have almost overcome us without it!.... [H]e was an army benefactor..., and will always be remembered most lovingly, by his old companions in suffering and peril.[8]*

In agreement with Goodloe, surely, would have been James Dinkins. He served both as a private in the 18th Mississippi and as an officer under General Nathan B. Forrest. To Dinkins' knowledge, every company had "one or more men or boys who everlastingly had some surprise for you. They were the comedians who furnished life and fun for the balance of the crowd. These fellows invariably made good soldiers; and by their pranks and jokes made the other men forget their troubles and dangers, too. They were meat and bread when we were hungry; and they gave us new life on the march when we were worn out. Every old soldier will recall,...the names of the men...who furnished the fun, and who always had some poor fellow on the rack."

One of Dinkins' own memories was that of a Yazoo City private in the 18th Mississippi, who could crow like a rooster and bark exactly like a dog. "I have known him to quicken the step of the whole brigade and put them all to laughing and talking. Just before day, on occasions when we had been marching all night, he would crow like a young game cock, and then you would hear him imitate a big old [rooster]. This would wake up the dog, and he would begin."

In a similar vein, Lieutenant Bromfield L. Ridley collaborated how the army had some of the finest mimics in the world. "Let one cackle like a hen," he voiced, "and the monotony of camp is broken by the encore of 'S-h-o-o!' Then other cacklers take it up until it sounds like a poultry yard stirred up over a mink or weasel. Let one bray like an ass, others take it up until the whole regiment will personate the sound, seemingly like a fair ground of asses."[9]

Artillery ordnance officer Frederick Colston, of General Longstreet's Corps, Alexander's Battalion, would have agreed with the above. He explained: "It seemed that the very privations of our service added to our gaieties. The fun and jokes always rose superior to cold, hunger, and fatigue, and seemed to mitigate their severity. It was certainly a happy diversion in the terrible hardships that we had to endure, and a visitor to a camp or an onlooker at a march might think us the happiest of men."

Lieutenant Colston knew firsthand of what he spoke. During the Gettysburg Campaign he had an opportunity to visit an aunt in Martinsburg, West Virginia, who provided a bath, a bed for the night, and a chance to have his uniform cleaned and brushed. He even obtained a paper collar for his coat, and all in all was pretty much "fixed up." In the morning as Colston waited for his battalion out on the main street, he was spotted by the passing Texas-Arkansas brigade of General Hood's Division. One of the dirty, dusty Texans could not resist a comment and called out: "O jiminy, don't he look nice? [To his comrade], John, throw a louse or two on him." Colston said he joined heartily in the laugh that followed.[10]

Captain H. W. Henry, Company K, 22nd Alabama, identified "[t]he cheerful humor of some comrade whose peculiar way of looking at things and manner of expressing himself made him a mascot in the company." Illustrating just such a man, he described a "boyish little fellow, with a whining voice, who always took things very seriously and never was guilty of laughter...." On one occasion when an order was read offering to give furloughs to soldiers who distinguished themselves in battle, he quipped: "Yes, but you are more likely to get thrown into the [burial] trench than to live to get it if you go about distinguishing yourself." At another time, when the company was moving past a female boarding school, the girls all came out and gave the men a hearty welcome, cheering and waving handkerchiefs. Captain Henry heard the piping voice say, "You are too late, gals. Chicken pie and waving your handkerchiefs got us into this thing; now show us the way to get out."[11]

The everyday humor of the Confederate soldier came in many forms. It could even get a Reb out of trouble, as we see when a private of the 5th Virginia Infantry stole a skillet from a fellow soldier early in the war. To disguise his misdeed, the thief snapped off the handle and rubbed burnt grease over the broken part. The true owner found it anyway, and turned his comrade over to the colonel. When asked what he had to say in his defense, the prisoner answered that he was positive the skillet was his, because his mother had just *sent it to him in a letter.* The colonel immediately released the accused from arrest, and ordered him to quarters, saying: "A man who can deliver as ready a lie as that will make a good soldier."[12]

Often it was just such a comment, made by a private soldier at the right moment, that gave the perfect impact to a story, like the time Tom Kirtley of Parker's Virginia Battery was struck in the leg by a piece of enemy shell. The blow knocked his wallet from his pants pocket onto the ground. "Well," said Tom, "I always thought the Yankees was mighty sharp fellows, but I didn't think they could pick a fellow's pocket a mile off!"[13] Then, there is the one about the soldier who left camp one day to visit a nearby town. Upon his return, he was asked about its merits. The wag quickly replied that he had seen only two people: "One was winding a Waterbury watch and the other had the itch."

Consider the "slip up" made by Colonel Bennett of the 14th North Carolina, when he witnessed a bullet strike one of his regimental officers in the mouth at the Battle of Spotsylvania. As he surveyed the damage, Bennett remarked: "I know your tongue will be glad as it will get a long-needed rest."[14]

Understandably, such characters became legends. But it was not only the soldier in the ranks who could let a *bon mot* fly. Some of the best "one-liners" of the war years came from prominent, ranking Southern officers, such as this one from General Thomas J. "Stonewall" Jackson. Upon hearing that his adversary, Yankee General John Pope headed his dispatches, "Headquarters in the Saddle," Stonewall commented that it was "strange that a General would have his headquarters where his hindquarters ought to be."[15]

General Jubal Early was certainly not one to be left out of a contest of wits. He once voiced the theory that if Plymouth Rock in Massachusetts had landed *on* the Puritans, instead of the other way around, "we would never have had [this] damned hell fired war" to begin with.[16]

Even in the thick of battle or on retreat, some "silver-tongued" Rebs never lost their comedic ability. Robert Stiles, who had formerly been a lieutenant of artillery in Cabell's Battalion, once saw a demoralized soldier so frightened that he was running from his proper position on the battle line. The terrified man, ordered to halt, even made a flying leap over the musket of a provost guard threatening to shoot him. But with all that, the scared fellow still managed to call back as he skedaddled: "Give any man fifty dollars to halt me, but [I] can't halt myself!"[17]

Captain Dickert had a similar encounter with a slightly injured officer who was fleeing the battlefield, "at such a gait as only fright could give." When asked if he was wounded, he answered, "Yes, my leg is broken in two places." Likewise, at the Battle of the Crater a few men of the 17th South Carolina, after the initial explosion of the Yankee mine, became panic stricken and were retreating for dear life. One officer, a normally staunch lieutenant of Company E, was seen sprinting to the rear at a high rate of speed, without hat, coat or shoes. After a few moments he came to his senses and cried out, "What! Old Morse running!" and immediately returned to his place on the firing line.[18]

Soldiers did not always have the last word. Periodically, Southern civilians were able to impress the army with a sharp shot of subtle humor. In one case, Tennessean Bennett Chapman was on scouting duty in an area of Virginia that had been pillaged bare to the bone by both sides. Forage was very scarce, but one day his company of scouts managed to find a small amount of corn with which to make a meal. They asked Chapman to take it to a mill in the vicinity to have it ground into meal. This accomplished, Chapman noticed that the miller had not asked for payment, and being an honest man he notified the miller that he might have made a mistake and forgot the charge. "No," the man replied, "I never toll my own corn."[19]

Confederate humor came in all forms. Examination of some common categories allows a view of the personalities who made and enjoyed the fun. At the same time, it offers a glimpse of what it was about army service in the 1860s that Southerners found enlivening.

"Characters"

Peculiar or oddball "characters," much like Dave Montgomery mentioned earlier, were always popular. South Carolinian D. Augustus Dickert documented several. For instance, he wrote of a curious private nicknamed "Mucus," after the Latin word for "calf," who constantly fell down, anytime, anywhere, and for no apparent reason. He fell over while marching, while standing in the road leaning on his rifle, or while in his tent. Mucus once tumbled from a boxcar backward into a ten-foot ditch, but he rarely, if ever, got hurt. He invariably blamed somebody else for his fall, saying such things as: "I wish the damn car would go on or stand still, one or the other." This, even though the boxcar had been perfectly still. Another time Mucus walked out of ranks to the edge of an abutment on a river bank and looked over. Sure enough, he toppled fifteen feet down into the river. When he pulled himself out, he exclaimed: "If I knew the damned man who pushed me off in the water, I'd put a ball in him." Of course, no one had been within twenty feet of him at the time. "How deep was the water, Mucus?" someone called out. "Deep enough to drown a damn fool, if you don't believe it, go down like I did and try it."

Another of Dickert's specimens was Jim George, described as a "shallow-pated wit," and a "good, jolly fellow," who was generally harmless. But in certain situations Jim's tongue had raised him to almost mythical status in his regiment. For example, during the fight at Yorktown, Virginia in 1862, Jim's captain, Chesley Herbert, saw him loading and firing his weapon for all he was worth, aiming at already wounded Federals. The captain remonstrated Jim, telling him he should not shoot injured men. In reply, Jim asked, "What in the hell did we come to the war for, if not to kill Yankees?"[20]

"Catch phrases"

"Bywords" or "catch phrases" were very popular during the war period, and every unit became partial to particular sayings at various intervals during the four-year conflict. These expressions usually sprang from something simple. All it took was for a single innocent Rebel soldier to get one going, and it soon took on a life of its own.

One of my particular favorites was quoted to a Pennsylvania tavern owner in Gettysburg during the occupation of the town between July 1 and 3. A group of tough, war-weary Confederate infantrymen had gone into a hotel near the center of town and demanded liquor. When told it was all gone, one of the Rebs said to the barkeep: "That will do for the marines, but it's too thin for us. We have travelled."[21]

William W. Blackford, who went to war as a private in the 1st Virginia Cavalry, documented his first "catch phrase" when General George B. McClellan, commanding the Union forces during the Peninsula Campaign of 1862, ordered a "change of base" for his army. "Changing one's base" became a byword among the fun-loving Rebel troops to signify discomfiture or defeat. According to Blackford, if "two dogs fought and one ran, the men cheered and shouted, 'Look at him changing his base;' if a man fell in the mud, his comrades would laugh and ask him what he was changing his base for; or if the rain flooded the place where they were sleeping they would say, 'Come, fellows, let's change our base.'"[22]

In another example of a phrase "catching on," a soldier on picket rushed back to report to his captain that he saw Yankee artillery moving into position opposite their camp. The frightened private began his story with, "Captain, I am no sensationalist, but the enemy are planting a battery on the hill over there." The captain immediately ordered out the company, and all advanced in a skirmish line to attack the supposed guns. On getting closer, the "battery" proved to be an old-fashioned farm cart which a local citizen had driven up and turned around with the tail-board toward the camp. As can be imagined, "I am no sensationalist" became a "byword" classic.[23]

One phrase that seems to have been unique to the Rebel army was something akin to, "We've come out here for a purpose, and don't propose fooling around." One writer put it thusly: "Johnny was remarkable for a studious application to the matter in hand."[24] In other words, we are here to do a job and we will do it and will not be put off.

Joseph B. Polley of the 4th Texas Infantry told the story of a friend, Jack Sutherland, who at the Battle of Chickamauga, went forward to fight near a lone Mississippian. The Mississippi soldier welcomed him and said, "Help me send some of those Yankees over yonder to kingdom come, will you?" Sutherland, all business, replied: "Of course I will, that's just what I came for."[25]

Likewise during a skirmish near Fishing Creek, Kentucky in January 1862, the major of the 20th Tennessee Infantry, Patrick Duffy, noticed his men were becoming a little nervous at the screeching enemy artillery shells and hissing bullets. To calm the troops, Duffy gave them what was essentially a hard fact: "Boys, 'tis pretty rough but that is what we are here for."[26] And consider Colonel Andrew J. Grigsby of the 27th Virginia, who after being wounded in the shoulder on July 1, 1862 near Malvern Hill, Virginia, was asked by one of his men, "if it hurt?" "Yes, damn it," was his pointed answer, "it was put in there to hurt."[27]

On the battlefield of Sharpsburg, Maryland on September 17, 1862, Sergeant Bill Andrews was speaking to a wounded color-bearer of the 1st Minnesota. The Yank made reference to the fighting and affirmed, "You boys seem to be getting the best of it." Andrews responded somewhat laconically that, "we had come there for that purpose."[28]

The most famous "byword" of the war, of course, was the ubiquitous "here's yer mule." The whole story and import of those few words likely began as here described by a Texas infantryman named John W. Stevens. The incident took place on or about the 28th of June 1862 near the battlefield of Savage Station, Virginia:

An old farmer who lived near by, and had weathered the storm (battle) came stalking through our camp, inquiring for a certain mule, with long ears, a glass eye, and a swab tail; he inquired of several of the boys as he passed through the camp about his mule, finally some one away off in another direction would yell out to him "Say, say there; mister say, here's your mule," and away he would go to find the man that had seen his mule; but of course he never found the mule. Then some one would hail to him from another direction: "Say mister, here's your mule"—and, then some one would call, from an opposite direction, "Say mister, here's your mule." But the poor old man could never find the man that called to him—he was always somewhere else. Then a hundred or more voices would start up in a sort of a chant:

> *Old man, old man*
> *Don't be made a fool*
> *I'll tell the truth as best I can,*
> *Jeb [Stuart's] got your mule.*[29]

This expression became such a common phrase for any and everything in the Confederate army, that after a while it had no direct connection to the original meaning. For instance, a soldier retreating during a battle might yell as he ran, "Here's your mule!" It could mean all things, or it might mean nothing.

Another use might be employed when an unpopular officer rode past a column of troops. He would soon hear someone in the ranks shout out to him for no particular reason, "Here's yer mule!" So obviously, to the common soldier it was a state of mind, a way to express every emotion felt by every man in the Southern army.

Another good illustration has come down to us from Private Sam R. Watkins of Co. H, 1st Tennessee Infantry, while near Romney, Virginia in the winter of 1862. A man named Schwartz in Co. E, a "full-blooded Dutchman" who was known as "God-for-dam," began firing at the Yankee pickets during a full-blown snow storm. As he shot off his musket, he would yell out at the top of his voice, "Here is your mule," but Watkins said it sounded more like, "Yer is yer mool!"

Private Watkins later recounted another incident, this time at the Battle of Missionary Ridge in Tennessee in 1863. As the Confederates began to retreat from their position on the ridge, General Braxton Bragg rode up to the troops in an attempt to rally them. He called out, "Here is your commander," in hopes of inspiring the breaking Southerners. In reply however, the soldiers "hallooed" back, "Here is your mule," as they continued to run for the rear.[30]

A slight variation to this famous "catch-phrase" was pointed out by William M. Owen of the New Orleans Washington Artillery. It began in their Virginia camp near the Potomac River in late October, 1861. Instead of a mule, however, the byword was an imaginary person:

> That mythical personage, "Bolivar Ward," seemed to have arrived today, for he was much inquired after. It was a camp joke to send some credulous fellow off on a wild-goose chase to find a letter or package from home, or something imaginary, said to be in the possession of "Bolivar Ward." The information would probably emanate from the guard-house, and the victim would be sent to the extreme end of the camp for "Bolivar," only to be sent to the other extreme, all the while asking every one he met, "Have any of you fellows seen Bolivar Ward?"—"Oh, yes! I saw him at the picket rope," one would reply. At the "picket rope" he had been seen at the Colonel's quarters, and back he would go; after wasting his precious time for a few hours, he would discover the "sell" and "acknowledge the corn." This afforded great amusement, and it became a standard reply to all inquiries such as "Where's the skillet?"—"Bolivar Ward has it."—"Where's the water-bucket?"—"Bolivar Ward has it."[31]

The Irish

The Irish quickly became a "constant" in the humorous personality of Southern army life. Not only were many Irishmen just plain "funny," they took pride in that envied reputation. Their perfection in these matters greatly helped themselves and all non-Irish comrades to keep in a perpetually cheerful state. In just about any memoir written by an ex-Confederate, good Irish comedy is present, and the jokes were not always on the Sons of Ireland themselves.

The most prevalent humorous references to the Irish appear to be much like the tale of "Tim," a private in Captain Pat Griffin's company of the 10th Tennessee Infantry, a regiment composed mainly of Irishmen. During the Fort Donelson Campaign in February 1862, the 10th came under enemy fire for the first time. Tim, who had no notion of the sounds bullets made, thought the unfamiliar buzzings he was hearing were mosquitoes. When he told this to his companions, someone let Tim know that the noise was not from insects, but Yankee lead. Tim, taken aback by this turn of events, exclaimed, "O God! we will all be kilt!"[32]

One of the most quoted stories on Irish wit, which can be found in several sources, is a simple one, and goes something like this: The battle had grown hot and deadly, and somewhere along the line, a soldier has a finger shot off by enemy musketry fire. He is making an awful fuss about it, crying and yelling with pain. Nearby, an Irishman calls over and upbraids him for being such a baby, saying, "Dry up, you bloody booger. A man yonder has just lost his head, and divil the word you hear out of him."[33]

Another oft-told story from period literature concerns a Confederate Irishman and prisoners of war. The hero in this case came "back from an expedition against the enemy, driving three Union soldiers in front of him. When he delivered up the prisoners, General [John H.] Morgan complimented him upon his gallantry. 'How on earth did you capture three men single-handed?' inquired the admiring cavalry leader. 'Oi surrounded 'em,' the Irishman replied."[34]

Commentators on Confederate army life in the 1860s viewed the Irish as capable of using picture-perfect expressiveness to describe a feeling or a scene, as in this one about a "Son of Ireland" after his first battle: During a fight with the Yankees, an Irishman was observed by one of his officers taking shelter from incoming projectiles instead of doing his full duty. After the action, the officer, "thinking to take the man down a peg, said: 'Well, Pat, how did you feel during the engagement?' 'Feel?' said Pat. 'I felt as if every hair on my head was a band of music, and they were all playing Home, Sweet Home.'"[35]

Hard to resist is the one about two brave Irish ex-Confederates, Pat and Mike, who in peace time were attached, but not quite inseparable. One day in passing an open coal mine-shaft, Pat fell into the dark pit. Mike was deeply grieved and called out piteously, "Pat! If you are dead, spake to me!" The fall was severe but not fatal, and a response was returned: "I'm not dead, but I am speechless."[36]

Colonel William C. Oates, 15th Alabama, making a point to a story in his memoirs, retold one of the best. While a battle was in progress the general in command spied an Irishman fleeing from the field. The officer halted the man and then and there chided and abused him for his cowardly conduct. The Irishman responded with, "Ah! Gin'ral, I had rither be a coward for the next two or three hours than to be a corpse for the rist o' me life."[37]

Who can argue with that kind of logic?!

General Jubal Early, known for his enjoyment of a good anecdote, had his own brush with the quick wit of the Irish, even *while* "being hung by his own petard!" At the Battle of Fredericksburg, Early was seeking information and wanted to ascend to the crest of a hill to make observations. Leaving his horse in a thicket he went forward. A while later, the general encountered a "tight" Irish soldier staggering along coming from the same thicket. Knowing the man to be a good soldier he ordered him to come forward. General Early then promised to release the besotted fellow if he would tell where he obtained the liquor:

> *Pat was pretty drunk, but not so drunk but that he caught the words of General Early. Straightening up as best he could, he came to attention and saluting, said: "And did I hear yer honor say if I would tell ye where I got me whisky you would release me?"*
>
> *"Yes, that is what I said."*
>
> *"Faith, and yer honor would not be after fooling an old soldier?"*

"No; if you will tell me I will be as good as my word and let you go to your regiment."

"Well, Gineral, yer honor's self must know that as me and Tim Merony were bringing ammunition from the wagons just ferninst the hill, we saw a be-u-tiful "hoss" in the thicket, and while admiring the fine crather we spied the neck of a bottle sticking out of the saddlebags-the sight of which niver the son of my mither could withstand. Sure, the Gineral will not begrudge a drap to a poor old soldier fighting for his country."

He was promptly [released].

Royal W. Figg of Parker's Virginia Battery knew one of the best foragers in the Army of Northern Virginia. He was a Louisiana Irishman named Patrick Brooks who had a great talent for "impressing" food stuffs. And rare for an artilleryman, Brooks always carried a rifle. The weapon was not to shoot at Yankees however, but was used for "domestic game" only, such as hogs, chickens and cows. Brooks had the Irish manner of "understatedness" too, as we learn in Figg's account:

> *It was said that one day he went into the yard of a farm-house, and, seeing a pig, he raised his rifle to shoot the "ferocious" brute, when the lady of the house rushed to the door, exclaiming, "Please, Mister, don't shoot my pig!" Pat with a look of injured innocence and dignity, paused a minute, and then said, "Oh, be off with you now! You are just after making me lose my aim!"[39]*

Because the Irish fought on both sides during the war, they were often criticized for destroying their own people. The North particularly condemned them, as Southern Irish soldiers were perceived to be supporting slavery, even while their own history was fraught with the desire to be free from British rule. Rebel Irishmen countered this by reasoning that their support reflected Ireland's cherished ideal of the right to self-rule and independence for any people who wished it.

British subject Colonel Arthur Fremantle, while visiting the Confederacy in 1863, made the mistake of confronting a Rebel from the Emerald Isle on that very subject:

> *I...made acquaintance with two Irishmen.... One of these men had served and had been wounded in the Southern Army. I remarked to him that he must have killed lots of his own countrymen; to which he replied, "Oh yes, but faix they must all take it as it comes." I have always observed that the Southern Irishmen make excellent "Rebs," and have no sort of scruple in killing as many of their Northern brethren as they possibly can.[40]*

Humorous stories of Irishmen, it is known, very often center around their fondness for the "wee drops" of any type of spirits, called by them "the sweet crathur" or "John Barleycorn." Cannoneer Edward A. Moore of the Rockbridge Artillery related this story of fellow batteryman Tom Martin. Martin had become angry at the captain for confiscating and destroying a supply of apple-brandy that had been brought to the camp to sell to the soldiers by another Irishman named Doran.

Greatly enraged at the "ill-treatment of a fellow son of Erin," and the loss of the precious fluid, no doubt, Martin got revenge by taking "French leave." As he made his way from camp, Martin soon came to the foothills of the North Mountain in western Virginia. "In the course of his journey," said Moore, Martin "stumbled on a stillhouse in one of its secluded glens. To the proprietor who was making a run of apple-brandy, and who proved to be 'a man after me own heart.' Martin imparted his grievances. 'I tould him,' said he, 'I hadn't a cint, but he poured me a tin [cup] chuck-full. With thanks in me eyes I turned off the whole of it, then kindled me pipe and stood close by the still. Ah! me lad how the liquor wint through me! In thray minits I didn't care a domn for all the captins in old Stonewall's army.'"[41]

"Humor as Pretense"

In recalling the Irish artilleryman who carried a rifle to shoot game, it brings to mind similar actions of Southern soldiers who used humorous pretense to justify stealing and killing farm animals belonging to civilians they met while campaigning.

Texan John Stevens admitted flat out that General E.M. Law's Brigade, while on the march into Pennsylvania in the summer of '63, "treated a flock of sheep about as badly," as most soldiers did fowls. He heard one man say that there were 95 sheep skins in General Law's camp, and "when some one spoke to [the general] about it, he said that no man's sheep could bite his men without getting hurt."[42] In like manner, a Georgian stationed near Lake City, Florida, attested to seeing numerous hog skins lining a farmer's fence near their old camp. He concluded it was the work of his own companions, for they had sworn that "they will kill any man's hog that tries to bite them."[43]

The stoic seriousness of anyone speaking the above words to a regiment of Confederate veterans, would surely have been interrupted by peals of laughter emanating from the ranks. Lieutenant B.L. Ridley knew this when he wrote that, "[in] camp, when all is still, the monotony is broken by some forager making a hog squeal. His fellows cry out, 'I'll kill any man's hog that bites me.'"[44]

"Slave Humor"

The Irish were not the only group of people who came under the watchful eye of rank and file Confederates from 1861 to 1865. The black slaves who lived in the regions occupied by Rebel forces, or were attached to the army itself, provided unlimited frolic fodder for the soldiers of the South. These slaves, too, like the Irish, often got the last laugh. A majority of slave oriented humor went something like the following.

Lieutenant Randolph H. McKim was a staff officer assigned to General George H. Steuart, and was present in the fight near Williamsport, Maryland, during the waning days of the Gettysburg Campaign. The artillery fire was especially heavy there, and a servant for one of McKim's fellow officers appeared on the scene during the bombardment. McKim remarked that the officer called to the man and asked: "Caesar, what are you doing here? Have I not ordered you always to keep in the rear when fighting is going on?" "Yes, Marster," replied Caesar, "I know you told me dat. But I declar fo' God. I'se look every whar on dis here battle field dis day, and I cyarnt find no rear."[45]

For a veteran, it was hard not to toy with the mind of an innocent bystander, whether he was a fellow soldier or a camp follower. All were equal game when it came to playing "dirty tricks." Artilleryman Royal W. Figg sketched a good tale which occurred on August 30, 1862, during the Second Battle of Manassas, when the men of Parker's Battery were going into bivouac after a long, tiring march:

> *As Billy Cogbill lay down, he noticed that the man next to him seemed to be sleeping soundly, although we had been in camp but a few minutes. Cogbill's suspicions were aroused. He shook the man, and found that he was dead. He wore the blue, and had been killed in these woods during the fighting on the previous day. Lieutenant Brown directed "Major," his servant, to wake up the supposed member of our battery [who was] asleep too near his horse. "Major" pulled the sleeper vigorously by the leg, which, to his utter consternation, gave way; whereupon he ran up to the Lieutenant, exclaiming, "I can't woke dat man, sah, dough I'se pulled his leg clean off,...!"[46]*

The common sense of one camp servant was long remembered by members of the 7th Virginia, as they moved into battle on the cold, frosty morning of December 13, 1862, near Fredericksburg, Virginia. David E. Johnston, peering into the mist, saw a lone figure coming toward the regiment just as the sun broke through the fog along the Rappahanock River:

> *Meeting a negro man loaded with blankets, canteens, haversacks and general baggage, puffing as if almost out of breath, with great drops of sweat as big as peas on his face—someone said to him: "Hello, Uncle! Where are you going?"*
>
> *His answer was, "To de r'ar, Sah!"*
>
> *Then the query, "To what command do you belong?"*
>
> *"Barksdale's brigade, Sah."*
>
> *"Is it running too?"*
>
> *"No, boss, it never runs, but I always do."[47]*

One of the best stories of this kind, and under the circumstances, one which proves the subject of the humor displayed a very rational mind, came from the pen of 3rd

South Carolina Captain D. Augustus Dickert. It occurred "in front of Chatta-nooga" on the morning of November 22, 1863, as his brigade, Kershaw's, went forward toward the scene of battle:

> On nearing the city, we were shelled by [Yankee] batteries posted on the heights along the way and from the breastworks and forts around the city. It was during one of the heavy engagements between our advanced skirmish lines and the rear guard of the enemy that one of the negro cooks, by some means, got lost between the lines, and as a heavy firing began, bullets flying by him in every direction, he rushed towards the rear, and raising his hands in an en-treating position, cried out, "Stop, white folks, stop! In the name of God Al-mighty, stop and argy!"[48]

"Nicknames, Jibes, and Rivalry"

By far, however, the most popular diversion of the Confederate soldier was the continuous teasing bestowed on each other. This primarily rose from the rivalry that existed between the various states which made up the armies, and between the different branches of service, especially infantrymen and cavalrymen. This rivalry, of course, extended to officers and civilians too, with the infantry appear-ing to derive the greatest pleasure from the discomfort extorted from all classes other than themselves.

This inter-state rivalry interested Tennessee Lieutenant Bromfield L. Ridley, who listed some of the nicknames that he heard used while in service. North Caro-linians were known as "Tar Heels" due to the great production of pine tar within the "Old North State." Georgians were "Goober Grabbers" for the peanuts, or "goober peas" they grew. Alabamians were called "Yellow Hammers" or "Yaller Dogs," because a portion of their regiments went to war in yellowish colored uni-forms. Louisianians were "Tigers," and South Carolinians were "Rice Birds," etc.[49] Ridley neglected to provide his own state's nickname, but at least one regiment, the 10th Tennessee, was called the "Peckerwoods," a winner in my book.

Virginians, so said Ridley, went by the unenticing title of "Tobacco Worms," but other sources presented the preferred nickname of "Sorebacks." John Casler of the "Stonewall Brigade's" 33rd Virginia Infantry, was familiar with that slan-derous *nom de plume* and explained it so: "We would ask the North Carolinians if they had any 'tar,' and call them 'Tar Heels.' They would reply that they were just out, as they had let us Virginians have all they had to make us stick in the last fight, and call us 'sore-backs,' as they had knocked all the skin off our backs running over us to get into battle."[50]

According to Major Smith of the 14th North Carolina, the term "sore-backs" had come into being during the Battle of Seven Pines in 1862, when General Daniel H. Hill, seeing a Virginia brigade led by General William Mahone afraid to attack, ordered the 30th and 14th North Carolina regiments to move *over* the cowering Virginians. "Step on them and go forward," said Hill, and naturally, ever afterward the Virginians bore the pseudonym "Sorebacks."[51]

One Virginia artilleryman even acknowledged the aforesaid insult. Royal W. Figg stated in early 1865 that, "at Gaine's Mill the Carolinians charged the enemy over the backs of the prostrate Virginians; hence the name 'sore-backs.'" He did not seem offended by it, but just reported the story to illustrate the humor of the men, and the soldiers' basic need to compete.[52]

But due to the respect infantrymen held for each other, rivalry in the ranks was most often reserved for cavalrymen. When they were absent, civilians and any unknown, unpopular or pretentious officers who happened by, received a full share of merciless pestering.

The British military observer, Colonel Fremantle, was so aware of the savage heckling handed out to fashion-conscious officers on the march, that he once admonished a visiting European to refrain from wearing an elaborate uniform, due to the "invariable custom of the Confederate soldiers, of never allowing the smallest peculiarity of dress or appearance to pass without a torrent of jokes...."[53]

One excellent explanation as to why infantrymen and cavalrymen were so prone to competition and confrontation, comes from Private Joseph Polley of the 4th Texas:

> *About the strongest feeling infantry and cavalry have for each other is that of contempt. Down in the bottom of his heart the foot soldier nurses an idea that his mounted comrades lack a great deal of doing their whole duty in killing and taking the chances of being killed, while from his elevation on the back of a horse your cavalryman feels himself a superior being, and looks down with an air of humiliating pity upon an arm of the service which must depend upon its own legs for transportation.*[54]

This prevalent idea that the cavalry was less likely to fight than the infantry, and could usually be seen running to the rear before a battle, was, in fairness, due because cavalry pickets manned the outposts of an army. Thus, they were the first men "driven in," during an attack, thereby creating the impression they were evading combat with the foe.

Virginian William H. Morgan added fuel to the fire when he voiced that whenever "the drummers and the cavalry were seen going to the rear, some one was sure to say, 'Look out, boys we are going to have a fight.'"[55]

A horse soldier himself, Lieutenant Howell Carter of the 1st Louisiana Cavalry explained it this way:

> *Why the infantry should ever attempt to ridicule the cavalry has always been a mystery...for the sensible ones must know that the cavalry service...is unquestionably the hardest branch—it has been said and it is really true that they are the 'ears and eyes of the army.' While the infantry and artillery are resting quietly in camp, the cavalry are on the outskirts keeping back the enemy, thereby giving the opportunities for rest and sleep.... [C]ommon sense ought to teach them that if it were not for these friends on horseback they would be harassed and annoyed all the time.*[56]

Another cavalryman reinforced this idea. As he was weaving his way through a column of troops, an infantrymen asked him how long it took "them things to grow out of a man's heels," (referring to his spurs). He replied: "If it wasn't for them things you'd lose your wagon trains."[57]

Good sense prevailing or not, the mounted solder was still badgered mercilessly by the lowly "web-foots," who in turn, were disparaged by the cavalry as "dough-boys," "foot-pads," "mud-mashers," and "infants." The cavalrymen themselves called these experiences "running the gauntlet."[58]

Artilleryman William Dame, argued that the point of the jokes and gibes at the cavalry was "their *supposed* tendency to be *'scarce'* when *big fighting* was going on." Dame furthermore claimed that General Daniel H. Hill once proposed to offer a "reward of Five Dollars, to anybody who could find a dead man with spurs on." But General Jubal Early did one better. Impatient at the conduct of his mounted arm, he supposedly threatened that, "if the cavalry did not do better, he would put them *in the army*."[59]

Generally though, the more typical taunts consisted of remarks calling the cavalrymen "Buttermilk Rangers," among other things, because of their proclivity to roam the countryside hunting up good things to eat and drink, rather than doing any fighting. Such comments as "No fight to-day, the 'Buttermilk Rangers' are going to the front," or "Lookout, the rangers are running from the Yanks; look out for a battle." "Jump down and grab a root, we are going to bust a cap!" "Ten thousand dollars for a dead cavalryman," etc. etc. These barbs could be heard up and down the ranks of marching infantrymen whenever mounted troops were in the vicinity.

And if by chance an infantry regiment spotted a wounded horseman, jocular comments might also be heard:

"Say, boys, there's been an accident; a cavalryman's been wounded."

"Poor fellow! He must be a raw recruit, for he didn't know that the first duty of a cavalryman is to keep out of danger."

"Maybe the Yanks crept up on him when he was asleep." And so on.[60]

These statements were pretty much one-sided, and were taken in stride by all concerned. And rarely, but periodically, it happened that a horseman got in a "dig" of his own. In one case, a rider was hailed by a "web-foot" who yelled: "Ten thousand dollars for a dead cavalryman." The trooper immediately halted his steed and retorted: "That may be all so, men; but, I tell you what, if this war lasts much longer, damned if I don't give ten thousand dollars for a live infantryman." Needless to say, this saddle warrior departed in peace, leaving the "dough-boys" in his wake of dust and the solemnity of the occasion.[61]

In truth, though, the infantry, or "knapsack-toters" won the prize in most of these friendly exchanges. It surely did on the afternoon a veteran soldier caught sight of a dashing-looking cavalryman trotting along the road bedecked in a considerable amount of gold lace and feathers. As he approached, the infantryman, leaning on the muzzle of his musket, eyed him quizzically. When the horseman reined up, the vet inquired: "Say, Mister, did you ever see a dead Yankee? Cause if you didn't, and you'll go along with us for about an hour, we'll show you one." Failing to elicit any response from the contemptuously dignified, silently staring cavalier, he continued, in a reassuring tone: "You needn't be afeered, Mister, 'cause there hain't none of our cavalry got killed yet, and I hain't never heered of but one of 'em gittin' hurt, and he was kicked while he was currying...his creeter." Naturally a yell followed, and the cavalier rode off, while the "infants" set their trap for the next poor fellow.[62]

The artillery was not immune to the taunts of the other branches of service, but from the sources which have survived, batterymen appear to have been subject to but little teasing, as compared to their brethren on horseback. Most artillery-aimed jests were of the kind related to an oddity within a unit. This could happen, say, when heavy mud and the poor condition of the animals made it necessary to attach three or four teams of horses to each gun, rather than the customary two teams. An infantryman noting this while footing it alongside the straining animals, might cry out: "Here comes the cavalry, but what's the gun tied to the tail for?"[63]

As previously noted, the cavalry sometimes repaid the "web-feet" in kind. One payback occurred when a troop of horse soldiers offered to ferry some infantrymen across a stream. But as the innocent "dough-boys" attempted to mount onto the backs of the horses from a high bank, the cavalryman sped away, dropping them all into the water.

Sadly, for the mounted arm of the service, these were infrequent and savored moments. One infantryman attested that for the most part, troopers had to vent their hurt feelings on "wagon-dogs," the men who remained with the supply trains and ambulances, due to sickness, feigned illness, or cowardice. Private William Fletcher of the 8th Texas Cavalry observed that "Rangers" like him, when passing a wagon train, often sang this song:

Come, all you wagon dogs, rejoice
I will sing you a song,
If you'll join in the chorus—bow wow wow;
When we go to leave this world,
We will go above with sheets unfurled—bow wow wow.[64]

The cavalry may have come under the guns of the infantry more than its share, but let anyone approach marching troops, or venture into a bivouac, clothed in a fancy hat, colorful attire, tall boots, or anything out of the ordinary, then it was, "Wearer" Beware! Sergeant William Andrews agreed, and said that soldiers would, in that scenario, immediately enjoy a joke at anyone's expense. "A beaver hat, umbrella, or duster makes them go wild. [I] would not put on a beaver hat and walk through camps for anything. It makes no difference how venerable or old a man is if he has on a churn [shaped] hat he certainly catches it from all sides."

Those tall beaver hats, shaped like butter churns, were also known as "beegums," and were clearly a favored target of humorous attack. Jack Hawkins, a member of Company A, 9th Louisiana, became famous for wearing this style of headpiece, and even got used to the teasing:

[I]...was very conspicuous on account of a hat I wore. It was made in Georgia, very heavy, and when it got wet I allowed it to run up to seed, making it the shape of a sugar loaf, very sharp and tall. The boys used to holler out,

"Yonder comes Petersburg; I see the steeple." "Come down out of that hat; I know you are there, see your legs sticking out." "Hello, hat! where are you going with that boy?"[65]

The common epithets fired at a man bold enough to wear such a contrivance as a "beegum," or a straw hat, or to be caught in a pair of absurdly tall cavalry boots, or gaudy uniform, were of a similar nature, only varied somewhat from unit to unit or among individuals. The following is a fair sample:

"Say, Mister, where did you get that hat? Have you got a rammer for it?"
"Come out of that hat; want to boil beans in [it]"
"Come out of that umbrel; I see your legs!"
"Come out of them boots, I know you're in there 'cause I see your ears a wiggling."
"Lordy, he's mine! I saw him fust...!"
"Ef I was a louse, I would swim the Mississippi River to crawl in his head!"
"Let me kiss him for his mother!"
"Put him in his little bed!" and so on, ad nauseam.[66]

Lieutenant W.A. Smith of the 14th North Carolina penned a story of this kind. It concerned his company, and a certain innocent staff officer accosted on a road in Virginia on May 3, 1862:

A spruce young man,...came along riding a good horse, nicely habited-wearing a cap made of coonskin with the tail hanging down on the side just behind his right ear; evidently very proud of his get-up and of his position—his ears were assailed by some humorist: "Git out o' that coonskin," "Sure you are thar, See your laigs and your tail sticking out," "Let's ketch the varmint; a mess of coon 'ud go right good—rations is scarce." "Oh, shaw, boys hit's too green to eat." "Well, anyhow, hit's a coon all-right, fer I kin smell it. Hit's jest out of hits hollow." The dandy could stand it no longer. Putting spurs to his horse he was soon beyond our company to be assailed probably by another.

An unusually long mustache could bring on like results, according to Smith. A clean shaven youth with an assiduously cultivated mustache came by his company one day, and for his trouble received this greeting: "Say, mister! Why don't yer swallow dem rats? What fer you chaw and chaw and chaw dem so long fer? I know you-uns eats rats fer I see de tails sticking out yore mouf."

Private Mercer Otey of the Rockbridge Artillery had a version of the above "rattail" tale. His account occurred on a back road in Maryland on September 5, 1862:

One aid-de-camp I remember well, whom nature had endowed with long curling mustaches, of which he was very proud, had the bad habit of continually stroking them with his gauntleted hand as he carelessly clattered along the column, perfectly indifferent to the distressing cloud of dust that the poor patient infantrymen had to swallow and snuff, so he was greeted with shouts of "Where did you get them mice, mister? Pull 'em outern your mouth. I knows they's there, for I see their tails a wiggling." etc.[67]

A straw hat and a white linen duster, worn on a hot dusty day by an officer on General Polk's staff, brought forth a hail of comments from a bevy of soldiers, all started by a tall Missourian, who opened fire on the fellow: "Come out of that flag of truce, [We] ain't going to surrender!" Then, "Come out of that straw pile, we see your legs," and on and on, until he beat a "hasty retreat."[68]

To make matters worse, it never failed that some "web-foot" would saunter up to the same beguiled officer, and with an innocent and sad countenance, would say: "Mister, don't get mad with that fellow, he is about half crazy and hollows at every damn fool that passes by here." This of course, brought forth merry peals of laughter from the lowly privates in the ranks, leaving the officer to gallop off, muttering, "This is a hell of a crowd I have run into."[69]

It did not happen often, but these staff officers, cavalrymen, or civilians in tall hats, sometimes evened the score with an insulting soldier. Sergeant Andrews confessed that once upon a time a courier wearing a stovepipe hat near Jacksonville, Florida got the better of a private named Dan McDuffie. When the courier rode by, the company started in on him. Then McDuffie jumped out of ranks and yelled to him to "come out of that hat. No use to say you are not up there, [we] see your feet hanging down," etc. McDuffie kept after the poor fellow demanding the tall "beegum." Finally the courier "wheeled his horse and dashed back to McDuffie, pulled off the beaver, taking his own hat out of it and presented the churn to McDuffie, wheeled his horse, and galloped away leaving McDuffie standing in front of his regiment holding [the] hat and looking as much like a fool as anyone I have ever seen. The boys certainly made the welkin ring as they tossed their caps in the air."[70]

One of the slickest retaliations of this sort was witnessed by David W. Johnston, 7th Virginia, in early 1862, as he documented in this narrative:

> In passing along the roads and through the towns and villages, if a citizen with a high silk hat appeared, these clowns [in our company] would call out: "Mister, come out of that hat; I know you are in there, for I see your feet!" Another would likely call out: "Mister, my bees are swarming; lend me your hat to hive them in...." Occasionally they were paid back in their own coin. An old preacher, white-haired, with a long white flowing beard, one day rode into our camp, when one of these wags called out: "Boys, here is old Father Abraham," whereupon the old preacher said: "Young men you are mistaken. I am Saul, the son of Kish, searching for his fathers asses, and I have found them." The preacher had won, and nobody enjoyed the joke better than the fellows who had been beaten at their own game.[71]

In conclusion, consider this thought by Sergeant Walter A. Clark, 1st Georgia Infantry:

> War is a terribly serious business and yet camp life has its humor as well as its pathos, its comedy as well as its tragedy, its sunshine as well as its shadows.[72]

So, let us investigate these words of Sergeant Clark, and seek out stories of "sunshine, humor and comedy."

*"I know not how the truth may be,
I tell the tale as 'twas told to me."*

1850-1861

Pillow's Plight

Tennessee-born General Gideon J. Pillow had seen much military service during the Mexican War, and came out of that conflict well known to the citizens of the U.S. His subsequent Civil War career, however, was not as glamorous. But as would be expected, in all phases of life he highly valued his reputation. Some years after his return from Mexico, a story about him was circulated, which, as it made the rounds, surely must have brought discomfiture to Pillow, unless, of course, he took it well and it just made him laugh.

What happened was this. In order to compliment the general, a Southern newspaper editor wrote a notice about him. Due to the error of the typesetter, however, Pillow was called a "battle-scared hero" instead of a "battle-scarred hero." On reading the article, an irate General Pillow stormed off to the newspaper office and demanded an immediate correction. The distraught editor promised a quick response in the next day's paper. Unfortunately, when that edition appeared, the offending lines then read: "bottle-scarred hero."

It is not known if any further correction was demanded.

1/477

Phew!

During the organization of the 1st Mississippi Infantry under Colonel John M. Simonton, the individual companies were ordered to consolidate at Iuka, Mississippi in July 1861. Prior to departure, each man of Company F was told to collect a week's rations to hold him over until the state or Confederate government began to supply their needs. An officer in this company, Lieutenant LeGrand J. Wilson, gathered his own food and later joined his comrades at Wall Hill, a village in Marshall County, Mississippi. But before Wilson left home, his father Robert had kindly offered a barrel of sauerkraut so that the men might have some vegetable food while in camp. When the preparations were completed about July 10, Company F started for Iuka from Holly Springs, "kraut" and all.

In a day or two, the men arrived by train at Iuka, but no plans had been executed to allow for the accommodations of the soldiers. Therefore the men were conducted to their camping ground and told to make themselves comfortable as best they could. The soldiers managed by hiring a wagon or two, and by hauling on their shoulders and backs most of the baggage and rations—all except the barrel

of sauerkraut. As there was no depot at the railroad siding, the heavy barrel was left sitting on the platform. Four days later Lieutenant Wilson remembered the sauerkraut. So for the rest of the tale, we had better let the lieutenant go on his own:

As soon as we got the camp arranged and tents up, I went for my barrel of kraut. We were getting tired of cold rations and we needed a change.... I started for it early in the morning, that we might enjoy it at dinner. As I drew near the corner of the street before turning to the depot, I met a man holding his nose and in a run, and just before meeting me he turned loose his nose, exclaiming; "Golly, what a stink!" "What's the matter friend?" "Go on," he said, "and you will find out." Another came round the corner, and as he turned loose his proboscis, he exclaimed bitterly: "Damn the man that brought that cabbage to town!" I didn't take the hint, but as I turned the corner the hint struck me full in the face. What a sight! The hot July sun had caused my kraut to ferment and burst the barrel, and it was foaming and fizzing, swelling and smelling. There was more cabbage than could have been crammed in half dozen barrels with a compress, and such a stench! I never smelt anything to compare to it. I never claimed that cabbage.

32/24

Flush 'Em!

Undoubtedly, sixty-five-year-old General William "Extra Billy" Smith was one of the most unique characters who fought for the Confederacy. A lawyer, congressman and governor of Virginia before the war, he got his nickname from the government mail contracts he acquired; each time his routes got longer, he requested "extra" money from the treasury. Having no military background, when Smith became colonel of the 49th Virginia in 1861, he took his army duties quite lightly, and never missed a chance to criticize regular army officers and their often strict, petty rules, which were enforced upon the new volunteer regiments.

For instance it was reported that Smith drilled the 49th near Manassas in the summer of '61, "sitting cross-legged on the top of an old Virginia snake fence, with a blue cotton umbrella over his head and reading the orders from a book. On one occasion he was roused by the laughing outcry, 'Colonel, you've run us bang up against the fence!' 'Well, then, boys,' said the old Governor, looking up and nothing daunted; 'well, then, of course you'll have to turn around or climb the fence.'"

In 1862 another story was passed around about "Extra Billy." During one of the battles in Virginia he was ordered to charge and carry the breastworks of the Yankees—but first he had to take his command through a tangled abatis of interlocked, downed trees which lay in front of it. According to the official army tactics of the day, this required the men to move rapidly and hold their fire until they were through the abattis. Finally, the regiment began its advance with Colonel Smith boldly leading the way, riding well ahead. The abatis was filled with Union sharpshooters and his men began falling around him as they ran through the hail of bullets. Bravely, the Virginians continued the attack, until at last they appealed to him. "Colonel, we can't stand this, these Yankees will kill us all before we get in a shot." It was all that was needed to be said. Smith's anger at the career Regular Army officers who had put them in this mess came exploding out: "Of course you can't stand it, boys; it's all this infernal tactics and West P'int tomfoolery. Damn it, fire! and flush the game!' And they did, and drove out the sharpshooters and carried the work."

38/111

Hell! Fire!

The fight at Manassas or Bull Run, Virginia, which took place on July 21, 1861, was not the first battle of the Civil War, but it was the first of the larger engagements. Our story however, centers around a skirmish which occurred nearby and a few days before, on July 17. That action was known as Blackburn's Ford, and happened on Bull Run creek, a place about two miles north of Manassas.

For most of the Southerners who participated in this little encounter with the Yankees, it was their first time under enemy fire. To say that all involved were tense and nervous would be an understatement. At one point in the skirmish, two companies of the 11th Virginia Infantry were ordered to the ford where the Federals were making it pretty "hot" for a Confederate brigade led by General James Longstreet. Soon after these two companies joined the fray, the 24th Virginia came double-quicking up to the ford, also to assist. The 24th was one of the units in a brigade led by Colonel Jubal A. Early, known as "Old Jube," one of the most eccentric and unusual characters ever to wear the uniform of a Rebel soldier.

Meanwhile, the rifle and artillery fire from the Union side of the stream was intensifying. As these untested, green units entered into combat for their baptism of fire, confusion reigned, and the jittery officers went about calming their men and settling them down to the job at hand. And as can be expected in the heat of a battle, even with well drilled troops, novice officers and men often forgot or ignored the strict tactical drills they had so recently learned.

For instance, to load any Civil War muzzle loading weapon, nine steps were required to properly make the gun ready to fire. But during combat, veterans naturally made these steps mesh into a few quick, smooth movements. However, the 24th was not then composed of veteran soldiers. So they rushed forward toward the Yanks, officers urging the troops to hurry, and Colonel Early encouraging them not to panic. Finally, as the 24th came into position, the order was given to load, which as already described, was a nine-step precise process which took time. As bullets begin to fly over his head, one of the captains of the regiment stepped out in front of his men and gave the official order, "Load in nine times—load!" "Old Jube" just as quickly, in his high-pitched, piping voice, exclaimed: "Load in nine times? Hell and damnation! Load in the most expeditious manner possible."

10/57

Captain Queasy

Samuel W. Hankins of the 2nd Mississippi Infantry related the following tale in 1912. Sam's version is my favorite, although this same general story appears in other sources and is attributed to other soldiers, including Colonel Cadwalader Jones, 12th South Carolina Infantry, and Colonel John B. Strange, 19th Virginia.

It seems there was a certain captain in the 2nd Mississippi who had a great fondness for oratory. According to Hankins, he would never let an opportunity pass without making a speech to his men. On July 21, 1861 during the Battle of Manassas, just before what would be their "baptism of fire," the energetic captain seized the moment to harangue his anxious command. The speech was one of the usual ones, in that the men were told they were here to do battle with the enemies of their country; that the Yankees intended to rob you of your property, and "to deprive you of your constitutional rights and privileges for which your ancestors had fought, bled and died. Now, men, it behooves each of you to stand firm without dodging...," etc., etc., etc.

Just then BOOM! a shell burst overhead, scattering deadly iron fragments in every direction. Down went the good captain on his face. Just as quickly, he rose from the dust, barely flustered, and continued his patriotic lecture. "Yes, men, you must stand firm and not dodge." BOOM! Another shell, and again down went their officer. However, he stood up promptly and resumed the speech, saying: "Yes, men, to be dodging and showing any kind of fear will be placing a stigma upon your character and upon those loved ones at home which time can never erase." BOOM! went a third shell, and once more the earth and the captain embraced. But on rising this last time he faced his Mississippians with a grin and said: "But you may dodge the big ones if you like; it was the small ones I had reference to. I will finish my remarks when this thing is over."

4/14 & 2/7/354 & 9/117

A Strange Story

Following the Confederate victory at Manassas in late July 1861, the 12th Virginia Infantry remained camped in the locality of the battlefield. Eventually the 12th, under Colonel John B. Strange, was brigaded with the 8th, 18th, 19th, 28th, and 56th Virginia Regiments, commanded by General George E. Pickett. Most of their days were spent in guard and picket duty, camp details, drill, and local marches to get the green recruits accustomed to the routines of army life.

On one particular day, as the regiment marched along with Colonel Strange mounted and in the lead, General J.E.B. Stuart appeared in the distance ahead, coming toward them on the same road. As Stuart passed by, he remarked: "It is strange—passing Strange." This brought on a laugh in the 12th, said Second Lieutenant William N. Wood, "akin to a yell."

And that little tale brings us to the antics of another colonel of the same brigade, Robert T. Preston of the 28th Virginia. Lieutenant Wood explained:

> Camp duty became more irksome, false alarms more frequent, and the picket duty on Mason's and Munson's hills gave exercise in abundance. Who does not remember the "Up the hill and down again and no blood spilt" of Colonel Strange? Or the "Attention, my people, fall in, them fellows [Yankees] are a-coming?" Or the more original command of Colonel Preston of the Twenty-Eighth, "Fall in Twenty-Eight, fall in!" and raising his voice as he exclaimed, "If you don't fall in I will march the regiment off and leave everyone of you behind!"

9/8,11

One For The Road

Like many of the old soldiers who had served in the regular U.S. Army prior to the Civil War, General Arnold Elzey was "quite fond of a dram." When liquor was available, he and his staff usually enjoyed it while gathered together in good conversation and friendship. One night, as the spirits flowed freely inside his tent, the general began to feel pretty liberal, and so summoned the sentinel who stood guard at his headquarters, and offered him a drink. After this act of kindness, Elzey and the other officers tottered off to bed.

Now, as it came to pass, this same sentry returned to duty about daylight on the following morn. His post was again at the general's tent. And remembering the enjoyable "gift" of the previous evening, he stuck his head through the tent flap, and cast his eye on Elzey, who was sleeping soundly deep in the land of dreams. But the peaceful scene did not move the thirsty man, who woke Elzey up exclaiming: "General! General! ain't it about time for us to take another drink?"

Elzey roused himself up, but was not in the merry mood he had been the night before. He immediately ordered the soldier to the guardhouse for his insolence.

And for months afterwards, the poor fellow was accosted daily by his comrades with the greeting: "General, General, ain't it about time for us to take another drink?"

31/19

I'm Out of Here!

The First Company, Richmond Howitzers was an artillery battery which was accepted into Confederate service in June 1861. Its first months under military authority were difficult for some of the members, especially the young men who came from well-to-do families and were accustomed to the comforts and abundance of civilian life. Robert Stiles recalled that the wagon train of the Howitzers, *alone*, was as large as one which an infantry *brigade* would have used later in the war. Many of the privates brought along their servants, as well as large traveling trunks, plus other refinements of home, such as personal wardrobes and even dozens of face and bath towels.

Eventually orders came to these men to send all excess baggage back to Richmond, and to reduce all non-essential property to a bare minimum. One wealthy private who possessed a very elaborate outfit was mortified. He protested; he even wrote an elegant note to his captain "resigning" his position in the company. It did no good. This "curled and scented gentleman" was forced to stay on, and soon became a superb soldier. And, in time, he laughed as heartily as anyone when, "in after years, at some point of unusual want and stringency and discomfort, some impudent rascal would shout out, 'Jim, old fellow, don't you think it's about time for you to resign again?'"

38/46

Oh, That Hurts!

A small engagement between Federal and Confederate troops occurred near the Greenbriar River in western Virginia on October 2, 1861. The Yankees advanced from the area of Cheat Mountain on a reconnaissance, and were met by a battery and several Southern regiments including the 1st Georgia Volunteers. The fighting was brief, casualties were low, but any military action fought only six months into the war was considered interesting and important to the participants involved. So important in fact, that the early reports written and turned in to higher headquarters often read like Caesar's defeat of the Gauls.

One newspaper editor ultimately must have become weary of these grandiose "communications from the front," and the tiring thought of having to print each one, and of seeing each commander vying to out-do the next. The editor was Jon M. Daniel of the Richmond *Examiner* and his pen was often critical and merciless. On the occasion of the above noted skirmish, and its subsequent written account, he cast ridicule at the incident, saying that, "there were more casualties from overwork and exhaustion in setting up type for that report than from shot and shell in the battle."

39/32

Foolish Question

Private Robert Stiles of the Richmond Howitzers broke his kneecap in a fall during the early part of the Battle of Ball's Bluff, Virginia, on October 21, 1861. Not wishing to have him miss the fighting, Stiles' gun detachment arranged to have an ambulance carry him from place to place as they moved about on the battlefield. When the battery took position, Stiles left the ambulance and took his post as gunner where he sighted the cannon before it was fired.

The ambulance was driven by a "half-witted youth" named Benjamin Grover, who had been employed by the battery for that sole purpose. As Stiles was getting out of the vehicle for the third or fourth time that day, and was preparing himself to hobble painfully up a hill to take his place at the gun, he remarked to the driver, "Grover, why don't you go up yonder with me to fight? You are better able to do it than I am." "Yes," said he, "but there's a differ." "Well, what is it?" Stiles asked; "What is the differ?" "Why," said Grover, "You see, you 'listed ter git killed and I 'listed ter drive a avalanche."

38/63

Too Cheap to Live With

The 14th North Carolina Infantry went into winter quarters during October 1861, in the vicinity of Burwell's Bay on the James River, Isle of Wight County, Virginia. The camp was about 10 acres in size, and after building log huts, the men passed the time in the normal duties and entertainments of soldiers everywhere.

One enjoyment of the cold fall nights was to contemplate the question of why the war had started. One evening a group of officers had gathered around a camp fire and were talking on just that particular subject. Present in this circle of men was Captain Zebulon B. Vance of Company F, the "Rough and Ready Guards" of Buncomb County, North Carolina. For a time Vance held his thoughts, taking no part in the discussion, as he sat, leaning over with his head in his hands, listening to the others' opinions. Finally he was appealed to for his say. Rising from his camp stool and straightening up, Captain Vance said:

> Well boys, I don't know the cause of the war, but I knew it was bound to come. I was in congress last year and one day three members of congress from New England and myself left the Capitol together and were walking along Pennsylvania Avenue. We passed a saloon and the member from Connecticut asked us to take a "snifter." Nothing loath, in we went. The bartender gave prompt attention. Our host turned to one and asked, "What will you take?" Answer, "I will take a Tom and Jerry." "What will you take?" Reply, "A mint julip." Then addressing me, said, "What will you take?" I said, "Whisky straight," for, boys, that was what I was raised on in the mountains. We tipped our glasses to our host, drank and chatted. Our host pulled out his wallet and paid for his own drink and left us to do likewise. No, boys, I don't know the cause of this war, but I knew then it was bound to come, for we couldn't live with such a damn set."

29/30

Blown Away

Private William G. Stevenson of Company B, 2nd Tennessee Infantry, had reluctantly joined the Confederate army in April 1861. His regiment was made up of mostly Irishmen, a rough and tumble bunch who had worked in towns and on boats along the Mississippi River.

The seventh of November was an important day for Stevenson and his comrades, for it was the first time they were engaged in combat with the Yankees. The battle was called Belmont, and it was fought in Missouri against the forces of General U.S. Grant. During the fight, as in most battles, but especially the earlier ones, confusion was a fact of life. The men and officers were untested, the ground unfamiliar. Stevenson and his Irish compatriots were scared and excited, and many were not use to their weapons. As an example, at one point, a "Hibernian" officer or non-com near Stevenson, called out to his men: "Illivate your guns a little lower, boys, and ye'll do more execution."

But another incident really caught Stevenson's eye, and even in all the turmoil, was remembered for its humor:

> *There was a curious little Irishman in our company, nicknamed "Dublin Tricks," who was extremely awkward, and scarcely knew one end of his gun from the other, [and] furnished the occasion of [an] outburst of laughter, just when the bullets were flying like hail around us. In his haste or ignorance, he did what is often done in the excitement of rapid firing by older soldiers: he rammed down his first cartridge without biting off the end, hence, the gun did not go off. He went through the motions, putting in another load and snapping his lock, with the same result, and so on for several minutes. Finally, he thought of a remedy, and sitting down, he patiently picked some priming [powder] into the tube. This time the gun and Dublin both went off. He picked himself up slowly and called out in a serio-comic tone of voice...,*
> *"Hould, asy with your laffin,' boys; there is sivin more loads in her yit."*
>
> 35/54

"Ahhhh...!"

No collection of soldier stories would be complete without including one having to do with "bodily functions." During a portion of the winter of 1861-1862, the 4th Alabama Infantry was camped near Dumfries, Virginia. While at this post, one of the officers of the regiment became sick with yellow jaundice. He was Lieutenant William F. Karsner of Co. H; a "boon companion and a brave and gallant" fellow, *when well.* However, when taken ill, Karsner became a perfect nuisance to be around—irritable, quarrelsome and melancholy.

Robert T. Cole, of the 4th Alabama, has left us the explanation of what finally cured the lieutenant, who, while confined in the hospital, had declared that the jaundice would kill him, preventing him from ever seeing his dear mother again:

Wm. Karsner, 4th Ala.

> *All our efforts to cheer him were perfectly exhausted without the least effect in quieting him. When his malady became*

somewhat complicated, though not at all serious, the nurse,... came in smil-
ing and stated that the surgeon had ordered him to perform an operation on
Lieutenant Karsner. When the nurse displayed the instrument which he was
to use, Karsner, having a very vague idea of its use, declared he could not sur-
vive such treatment. We begged and pleaded with him, stating that his only
chance of recovery was to comply with the instructions of the surgeon. Finally
he submitted. After the departure of the nurse, he became very quiet for half
an hour or more and peace and quiet at last reigned in our ward, much to our
relief. One of the boys became alarmed at the unusual quiet of our patient and
remarked: "Do you suppose that operation has really killed him?" At the same
time he tip-toed gently over to Karsner's cot, to find him wide awake. He asked
in a very sympathetic tone: "Lieutenant, how do you feel now?" "Oh,"
Karsner said, "God bless enemas, when I recover I shall certainly take one
every morning."

47/36

1862

Dead Reckoning

Sometime during the first months of 1862 Corporal Joseph B. Polley and his
comrades of Co. F, 4th Texas Infantry were ordered to serve their share of picket
duty near Cockpit Point, Virginia, on the Potomac River. Their captain, Edward
Cunningham, assigned one post to Polley, and to privates Charley Brown and
Berman Gabbert, a German, or "Dutchman" as he was called. So, on a dreary
winter day they trudged through the snow and mud to their assigned position, and
made themselves as comfortable as circumstances would permit in such a miserable out-of-the-way locality.

That evening the three dispirited men were visited by the captain. He informed
them that since it would be very inconvenient for an officer to tramp from the
warm fire at the picket reserve to their post, they were expected to wake each other
up when it was time for guard change every three hours. Having no way to tell
time, this unexpected situation presented a problem to the unhappy trio. Polley
filled in what happened next:

"Bu-bu-but, Gabtain," chattered Gabbert,... who... was then on post,
"how—how—how vill ve know ven der zwei hours is oop?"
"Oh, you can guess at them, I reckon!" responded the officer, who turned
on his heel and made what he thought was a beeline for camp.
Neither of the shivering monuments of man's inhumanity to man whom he
left behind felt in the least inclined to apprise him that he was proceeding in
the wrong direction, and he had not gone fifty yards when he stumbled over a
hidden log and fell headlong into a muddy branch. Rising to his feet, he sput-
tered entreatingly, "Say, boys! Which way is the camp from here?" "Oh, you
can guess at it, I reckon!" I answered.

20/25

"Duffed"

Soldiers rarely let a chance go by to take a friendly "jab" at civilians they met along their routes of march. It was a time-honored tradition, probably dating back to the fighting men of the Assyrian, Greek, or Roman armies of the past. And in these encounters the military side usually prevailed, as they had their multitudes to draw from, for "wags" and "wits" were as numerous as fleas, and each regiment or battery had its own share of these comical characters.

One of the most common queries or veiled insults dished out to the male inhabitants, was the pointed question, "Why aren't you in the service of your country?" or some similar inquiry. It was sure to win the roadside debate, as the "uniform" almost always had the upper hand in that department, and the civilian, embarrassed by his lack of patriotism, quickly beat a hasty exit—*except,* in the following exchange.

The Confederate Army on this occasion had had a reversal of arms and was making a retrograde movement. In other words, it was on a full retreat. Lieutenant William Wood, 19th Virginia, was plodding along with the rest of his unhappy comrades. He noticed that John Dodd of his company, also known as "Duff Green," had taken an interest in an innocent-looking country youth sitting on a fence along the farm lane that the army was using in its withdrawal. "Duff" was constantly on the lookout for this type of situation, and saw an opportunity for fun in the soft face of this lanky, lazy-looking "green lad" perched on the fence. So he inquired: "When are you going to jine the Army?" And quick as a flash came the reply, "When you fellows stop running."

The laugh was, of course, on "Duff."

John Dodd's discomfort serves as a reminder of the one about the small boy who was leading his donkey past a Confederate military camp. Seeing the pair, a couple of soldiers decided to have some fun with the lad.

"What are you holding on to your brother so tight for, sonny?" said one of them.

"So he won't join the army," the youngster replied, without blinking an eye.

9/31, 2/40/367

"No Room, Sir."

Athens, Alabama was the scene of a skirmish on May 1, 1862 between a portion of the 1st Louisiana Cavalry and a Federal regiment. In this action the Confederates were victorious; they pushed the Yankees back toward Huntsville, and captured their camp. In the report issued for that tiny engagement, Captain W. W. Leake of the 1st Louisiana was mentioned for his gallantry in leading Co. C through the fight.

Captain Leake, however, had a somewhat different version of the affair, especially when it came to his bravery. He later admitted that at one point during the contest, the bullets were flying by quite briskly, and the enemy and the 1st Cavalry began using all available trees for cover. His version of the affair follows:

Lt. Colonel James O. Nixon and [I] were behind the same tree. All of a sudden a gun fired close by and looking up [we] saw it was young [John] Beck of Company C standing out in full view of the enemy firing away as if he was shooting at squirrels. Colonel Nixon scolded him for such recklessness and peremptorily ordered him to get behind a tree. "I can't do it," said Beck. "Why not?" asked the Colonel. "Because the trees are all occupied by the officers."

So the lieutenant colonel called to Captain Leake to leave the tree, and they both stepped out, with the intention that neither of them would let Beck see them even look toward a tree again.

41/47

Well, Sort Of...

As can be expected, discipline in some Confederate army units was very lax early in the war. Privates regarded themselves as good as officers, and sometimes better—and often they were right. This situation was still somewhat true during the Shenandoah Valley Campaign in Virginia in the spring of 1862, when in late April, General T. J. "Stonewall" Jackson's army was camped in the vicinity of McDowell, and troops under General Edward Johnson occupied Shenandoah Mountain.

As it happened, shortly before the Battle of McDowell was fought on May 8, a soldier from a Georgia regiment was placed on one side of said mountain as a picket guard. The Georgian had thoughtfully brought along his fiddle to keep himself company during the long hours of sentry duty. On that particular day, General Johnson and two members of his staff walked up to this soldier while engaged in an extended examination of the outposts under the general's command. When Johnson approached, the guard was playing away on the musical instrument, and his musket lay harmlessly nearby, resting against an adjacent tree. General

Johnson, noting this lapse of military etiquette became very indignant, and asked the fellow what the devil did he think he was? The soldier, never ceasing his music, replied, "Well, sir, I suppose I am a sort of a picket. What in the hell are you?" "Well," said Johnson, who was a rough, seedy-looking individual, and often went about wearing no insignia of his rank, "I suppose I am a sort of a general." "Well," answered the Georgian, "wait till I get my gun and I will give you a sort of a salute."

25/53 & 31/229

Isn't It Obvious?

General Thomas J. "Stonewall" Jackson was generally strict on his army corps when it came to marching. So much so in fact, that his troops were nicknamed the "foot cavalry." But Stonewall was equally severe on straggling. He did all that was humanly possible to keep his men in the ranks, and would not allow them to leave the column for any but a serious reason. And likewise, Jackson expected his officers to correct this "evil," which, if allowed to get out of hand, could cause a force to dwindle away to nothing.

After one particularly hard day's march, and after the troops had gone into bivouac for the night, Stonewall sent the following note to General Early, one of his division commanders:

Headquarters 2d Corps A.N.V.

To Gen. Jubal A. Early, Commanding Division

General—Gen. Jackson's compliments to Gen. Early, and he would like to be informed why he saw so many stragglers in rear of your division today.

Respectfully,

A.G. Pendleton, A.A.G. 2d Corps

To which "Old Jube" promptly dictated and sent the following reply:

Headquarters Early's Division A.N.V.
To Col. A.G. Pendleton, A.A.G. 2d Corps
Colonel—General Early's compliments to General Jackson, and he takes pleasure in informing him that he saw so many stragglers in rear of my division to-day, probably because he rode in rear of my division.
Respectfully,
Jubal A. Early, Commanding Division

One officer said of this: "There was not another officer in the Army of Northern Virginia who would have dared to send such an impertinent note to Jackson, nor another, save [J.E.B.] Stuart, whose impertinence in sending it would have met with a laugh."

38/190

Shot Down

Just prior to the Battle of Seven Pines, Virginia, which began on May 31, 1862, the 11th Mississippi Infantry was ordered to join General William Whiting's Brigade. The 11th, even so early in the war, was known for its superior training and marksmanship, and General Whiting was very proud of this fact. Being stationed within the state of Virginia, the 11th, like all other Southern regiments, was expected to protect the property of its citizens. It was prohibited from stealing food, and from joining in on other similar depredations. Officers were therefore instructed to prevent or to report these acts immediately to their commanders.

One day, Colonel William D. Pender, who led the 6th North Carolina, of Whiting's Brigade, went to brigade headquarters to say that a hog had been killed within the lines of the 11th Mississippi. General Whiting inquired of Colonel Pender as to what evidence he had of this breech of military law. Pender answered that he had heard the report of a gun inside their perimeter, and then heard a hog squeal.

"I am satisfied that you are mistaken, Colonel," replied General Whiting, "when an Eleventh Mississippian shoots a hog, it don't squeal."

51/10

Root Hog or Die

It is a fact in the history of the War for Southern Independence, that Stonewall Jackson was victorious in battle on several occasions. For instance, he defeated various Union armies in the Shenandoah Valley of Virginia in 1862 almost with impunity. Stonewall's admirers have said that it was his skill as a military officer that won these victories, and that is certainly true. But many of his hungry soldiers believed that "necessity" was one of the ingredients of his success. In other words, they reasoned, Jackson *had* to defeat the Yankees as the only means by which he could feed his troops.

John Robson, a Rebel in the 52nd Virginia, illustrated this concept with a tale he had once heard. Here in his own words, is Robson's analogy:

> *It is related, on good authority, that "once upon a time" a traveler found a boy, with hoe and crowbar, hard at work digging under a big rock, and inquired what he was after. "Groundhog under here," was the sententious reply. "Do you expect to get him out?" asked the traveler. "Expect to get him!" said the boy—"got to get him; preacher be at our house to-day, and we're out of meat."*

The mention of General Jackson brings to mind an anecdote of his expertise at seizing Yankee supplies and the wagons that hauled the bounty. During the Shenandoah Valley Campaign of 1862, a company by the name of "Moffatt & McKnabb" of Wheeling, Virginia, made wagons for the Union Army. And generally every Monday, they shipped 75 of the vehicles to the Federals in the Valley, wagons that were often captured by Jackson's cavalry soon after their delivery.

Sometime during this period, a paroled Yankee soldier brought a letter to the offices of the wagon manufacturer. It was from the Rebel general himself:

Messers. Moffatt & McKnabb, Wheeling, Va.

Dear Sirs:
  I have just received your last consignment of wagons. I like them very much; but hereafter please make their tongues a little stronger, *as many of them are broken off when turned over to me. Respectfully,*
T.J. Jackson

22/50 & 52/96 & 2/19/520

The "Know Nothing" Party

One strong trait of Stonewall Jackson, which persists throughout many eye-witness accounts of his character, concerns his fanatical belief in keeping his military plans secret. The general told no one of his tactics, lest some person give away information which might help the enemy.

In late June 1862, prior to leaving their camps at Mount Meridian, Virginia, an order was issued from "Stonewall" to his troops. This directive instructed all soldiers to tell no one the names of their units or commanders, and in short, to answer all questions with feigned ignorance.

One day shortly afterward, Jackson happened upon a lowly private crossing a field, headed toward some ripe cherry trees. Attacks on these trees had caused much straggling by his men while on the march, and Jackson had not been able to keep it in check. So, here was a fellow of whom he could make an example. Riding up to this target of opportunity, the general inquired: "What division do you belong to?"

"Don't know," answered the miscreant. "What brigade?" was "Stonewall's" next inquiry. Again, "Don't know." "Well," persisted Jackson, "What regiment do you belong to?" thinking the he had found an answerable question. But once again, came the same—"Don't know." Then with some roughness of tone, the general exclaimed, "What do you know, sir?" The stoic Reb then looked up and said: "I know that old Stonewall ordered me not to know anything, and damned if I ain't going to stick to it."

The general turned away smiling, "at the extreme literal construction of orders which had saved the soldier from the punishment he had meditated for him."

30/73 & 20/48

Dodge 'Em!

Every old soldier was fond of a good yarn, especially one with humor that dealt with his own commander. And if the officer in question came out of it looking "more human," even when the laugh was on him, then so much the better.

Something of this sort took place during the Peninsula Campaign of 1862. It was at a time General Richard S. Ewell was told to move his division to Dispatch Station on the Virginia and York River Railroad, located east of Richmond, about half way to the Pamunkey River. Upon arrival, his troops destroyed a bridge and a train.

The next day, June 29, some men of Captain Elijah V. White's cavalry company, and Colonel Bradley T. Johnson's 1st Maryland Infantry, were searching along the Chickahominy River for signs of Yankee activity. Occasionally a shot was fired into the woods from a rifled cannon White and Johnson had brought along. By evening this gun was eliciting replies from several Federal batteries.

It so happened that about this hour, General Ewell rode up to get the dispositions of the Union positions from Colonel Johnson. By then the enemy shells were flying pretty plentiful around both officers. Ewell soon turned his horse, and remarked to his escort, "We'll go back now, boys!" The general and his party then trotted over a hill toward Dispatch Station. However, in so doing, they passed in full view of the Yankee line, who in turn opened their guns full force on the group. But just before reaching the nearby woods, a projectile passed between Ewell's head and his horse's neck, causing the general to make a sudden backward motion. He quickly recovered though, and righted himself up on his mount. The shot then struck a large pine tree about 20 feet from the ground, and cut it off so cleanly and smoothly that the upper part of the tree came down perpendicularly, and stuck in the ground beside the trunk. Seeing this, the general exclaimed, "Wasn't that beautiful; wasn't that well done!"

Yet in thinking back, some of his soldiers remarked that they did not know exactly whether Ewell had made reference to his "dodge" of the shell, or to the cutting of the tree, and they were afraid to ask.

30/79

The Band Need Not Apply

General Daniel H. Hill, a West Point graduate, Mexican War veteran, and Southern educator before and after the war, served the Confederacy with distinction in the years from 1861-1865. An officer who knew Hill, Captain William T.

Poague, once described the general as "brave, a stubborn fighter, extremely sarcastic, [and] disposed to make light of the other arms of service—cavalry and artillery—and [was] bitter towards 'Yankees.'" His preference was the infantry, which he considered to be the real fighters of the army.

Once when a member of one of the regimental bands in his command made application for a furlough, General Hill endorsed the document in this manner: "Respectfully forwarded, disapproved—shooters before tooters."

19/31

Food Fight

General John B. Hood's Texas Brigade felt proud of their exploits during the Battle of Gaines's Mills, Virginia, fought on June 27, 1862. The 4th Texas, of that brigade, was particularly complimented for being the first to break the Federal lines. The 5th Texas was commended too, for its part in capturing large numbers of prisoners from the 4th New Jersey and the 11th Pennsylvania.

During the latter episode, as hordes of Yankees began surrendering to the 5th, many Union officers insisted on tendering their swords to Major John C. Upton of that regiment, as a token of their submission. These Federals were so quick to give up their weapons, that Major Upton was compelled to lay down the frying pan he generally carried, in place of his own sword, so he had space to hold all the trophies presented to him.

Just about the time the twentieth or so sword was being handed over, Upton noticed a commotion down near the far end of the two captured Northern regiments. There, he saw a large squad of prisoners making an effort to turn around and escape back to their own army. The only person blocking their way to freedom was "Big Jim Ferris" of Co. B, and he stood there with gun in hand, unaided, endeavoring to intercept the progress of the Yanks.

"Springing upon a log, the armful of swords dangling about in all directions, Upton shouted, 'You John Ferris! What in hell and damnation are you trying to do now?' 'I'm trying to keep these damned fellows from escaping,' returned Big John, in a stentorian voice. 'Let them go, you infernal fool,' shouted back Upton. 'We'd a damned sight rather fight 'em than feed 'em.'"

20/58

Lee and Me

While on a rainy day march on or about June 30, 1862, during the period of the Seven Days' Battles, the soldiers of Company K, 16th Mississippi Infantry, had their first opportunity to get a look at their new commanding officer, General Robert E. Lee. Lee had taken command of the Army of Northern Virginia just a month earlier, after the wounding of General Joseph E. Johnston. On this particular day when Lee rode by the 16th, one of the members was absent. He was Private Winans Hoard, who had been off in search of a new pair of shoes. When Hoard finally returned, his comrades chided him for the lost opportunity of seeing their new leader. But Winans had not missed a thing, and answered them with this tale:

You saw him, did you? Why I have got you beat a mile. He stopped down the road where I was swapping shoes [with a dead soldier] and we had quite a conversation.

Well, tell us about it.

I had to hunt right smart before I could find a fellow with a good pair of shoes which would fit me. At last I found him right by the road. I made the swap and while sitting there putting on the shoes, a lot of horsemen rode up with ponchos and leggings on. The leader stopped and said, "Young man, you must go at once and join your command." I took him for some darned cavalry officer and answered: "That's always the way with you durned cavalry; when the fight comes on in real earnest, you skedaddle to the rear. And when we have gone in and won a sure enough battle and victory, you come moseying up with frills on, afraid we might get something off the battlefield, a pair of shoes for instance." The officer rode on without saying a word. But one of the staff stayed behind and spoke to me, saying: "Young fellow, have you any idea to whom you were speaking? Are you one of Jackson's men?"

I said, "Yes, and I catch myself not caring for the name of every durned cavalry officer who thinks he is some pumpkins because he can straddle an old horse and swing a rusty sabre." He said, "I thought you might be interested in knowing that you were speaking to General Lee." "Oh!" I said, "if that's General Lee it's alright and tidy, him and me are partners, though I never saw him before. He is the one that plans out a campaign and I'm one of the ones that fights it out." With that the officer laughed heartily and rode on.

55/87

Ned's (Basic) Needs

On July 4, during the Peninsula Campaign of 1862, the men of Confederate General John B. Magruder's command stationed near Yorktown, Virginia, found themselves on a tedious all-night march. Of course this "adventure" wore them out, and incited in the troops a craving for both a good breakfast and some much needed rest. One of the soldiers present on this midnight walk was Private Ned Phelps, a tall, erect, and handsome young fellow, and a member of the "Crescent Rifles," a company in the 1st Louisiana Infantry Volunteers. After spending some wasted time in the early morning hours foraging around for a bite to eat, the hungry Phelps eventually came to a farm in the vicinity of his regiment's encampment. What he did not know, however, was that his commander, "Prince John" Magruder and his staff had already taken over the premises, and were about to enjoy a good meal which had been cooked up in the farmhouse:

The General and staff had taken their seats at table, and were preparing to do justice to the viands set before them. Without ceremony Ned walked into the dining room, and, discovering a vacant seat, promptly took possession thereof. Magruder eyed him for a moment, and, with the lisping expression which the General affected, addressed Ned something like this: "Young man, are you aware whom you are breakfasting with?"

"Well," said Ned, "before I came soldiering I used to be particular whom I ate with, but now, I don't mind much—so the victuals are clean."

This answer so tickled Magruder that he immediately responded, "Young man, stay where you are and have what you want," which Ned did.

2/5/55 & 55/91

A Private Appeal

About a week after the Battle of Malvern Hill, on July 8, 1862, the Army of Northern Virginia began to move back to the vicinity of Richmond. Lee's entire army was exhausted after several months of marching and fighting on the Virginia Peninsula. On that march, General Stonewall Jackson and staff followed their own troops, starting after dark. Between 10 and 11 o'clock p.m., Stonewall was riding along, drowsy and nodding sleepily on his horse "Fancy" or "Little Sorrel," as he was generally known. As was his custom, Jackson trusted to that intelligent animal not to give him a fall. Staff member Lieutenant Henry K. Douglas, has drawn for us an excellent picture of what happened next:

More than once did we see his head nod and drop on his breast and his body sway a little to one side or the other, expecting to see him get a tumble; but he never got it. On this occasion our sleepy cavalcade at different times passed small squads of soldiers in fence corners before blazing fires, roasting green corn and eating it. Passing one of these, our staggering leader was observed by one of those thirsty stragglers, who was evidently delighted at the sight of a drunken cavalryman. Perhaps encouraged with the hope of a drink ahead, the ragged Reb jumped up from his fire and, brandishing a roasting-ear in his hand, sprang into the road and to the head of the General's horse, with, "Hello! I say, old fellow, where the devil did you get your licker!"

At that moment, related Lieutenant Douglas, Jackson woke up and asked all around if anyone had spoken to him. This gave the soldier a good look at the famous officer. After seeing who he had so rudely accosted, the man cried out: "Good God! It's Old Jack!" He then took a flying leap, cleared the road and a fence and scattered into the dark.

When the staff recovered from their laughter, they explained the situation to General Jackson. He was much amused, and immediately dismounted and took a half-hour nap.

33/115

Out of the Mouths of Little Rebs

Before the war began, there had been in the South citizens for and against the idea of secession from the Union. Many held to their original beliefs throughout the four years of bloody conflict. Others changed their minds, persuaded by circumstances not thought possible when the fever of patriotism had blinded them to the realities of a full scale, no-holds-barred, fanatical civil war.

The following, related in a humorous and quietly understated way, illustrates one of these "changes of heart."

The time was just after Yankee General John Pope was given command of all U.S. forces in the East (except those of General George McClellan). It was June 1862, and Pope began to maneuver his "Army of Virginia" against Robert E. Lee in Northern Virginia. The campaign was eventually a failure, as Pope was outfoxed by "Marse Robert" and his able lieutenants. So after the disastrous defeat at Second Manassas, Pope's troops were compelled to retreat toward Washington.

But General Pope was victorious in at least one aspect of the unsuccessful campaign. His army did create havoc among the civilian population. It destroyed and confiscated so much food, livestock, crops and other possessions, that a majority of the local populace was ready to declare the "heresy of secession," snuffed out.

Our story occurred near the once pleasant and prosperous town of Culpeper. Pope's men had been particularly thorough in their sweeps between that village and nearby Gordonsville, as well as the area southwest into the counties of Orange and Madison.

In this period of tribulation, a family near Culpeper was just sitting down to dinner when the Yankees descended on their farm. In fifteen minutes, not only had the officers and soldiers devoured the food on the table, but they had collected and carried away, "everything portable or eatable, livestock and all, indoors and out,..."

This foray evidently made a great impression on these poor people. We know because one of the Union officers present, who was much gratified at the scene, recorded that a little son of the proprietor claimed these sentiments for his father:

"Pap says he wouldn't vote the secession ticket again if he had the chance."

22/90

Oh, "Shoot!"

It would have been hard to top the Civil War military record of R. Lindsay Walker. He rose from battery captain in 1861 to brigadier general in 1865, while surviving 63 battles and smaller engagements in the process.

But during the fight at Cedar Run, Virginia, on August 9, 1862, Walker might have felt his days were numbered. That August day saw Colonel Walker serving as the chief of artillery for General A. P. Hill's Division, and at one point, the Confederate left wing had been thrown back by the Yankees and was in total disorder. Walker rode into the fray and "strenuously exerted himself to induce the stragglers to return to the fight." The task was not an easy one for the colonel, as the troops were demoralized by the suddenness of the Federal attack.

Soon Colonel Walker, due to his inability to stem the tide, became discouraged, then mad, so angry that he said he swore, and swore with "extraordinary vehemence and eloquence." In fact, on this occasion Walker surpassed all his previous performances, uttering volley after volley of hair-raising oaths.

In his struggles to save the line and get the men back to their posts, the colonel grabbed onto the collar of a passing straggler who had refused to stop at his order. Walker began "discharging at him a perfect torrent of curses, when, chancing to turn his head, he saw close behind him no less a personage than the oath-hating and sternly pious, General Stonewall Jackson:

"Jackson's aversion to profanity was proverbial in the army. It was known to excite his extreme displeasure. Colonel Walker therefore stopped abruptly, hung his head, and awaited in silence the stern rebuke of his superior."

It came in these words, uttered in the mildest tone: "That's right, Colonel—get 'em up!"

40/306

Heap Big Leap

During the August 9, 1862 Battle of Cedar Mountain, or Cedar Run, as the Confederates called it, Lieutenant Henry K. Douglas, as a member of Stonewall Jackson's staff, was told by the general to ride to General Richard Ewell with an order to move his men forward and attack. After delivering these instructions to Ewell, Douglas began his return trip over the same ground he had recently crossed. When he had gone half way he found himself in a dilemma. Yankee skirmishers had cut him off, and further progress back to General Jackson was blocked. The country being new and unfamiliar, Lieutenant Douglas next decided to return to General Ewell. But it was too late, the enemy had closed that avenue also, and a line of Federals was coming at him from that direction. The fields to his rear seemed open, however they were blocked by a very high fence. The time for contemplation ended though, as shots were fired and bullets came whizzing close over his head. So, having no other choice, Douglas made a rush for the fence. His horse, urged on with the spur and frantic with fright, did not hesitate. The animal made a desperate leap and landed on the other side, throwing a shower of ploughed earth into the air.

Later, when the battle had ended, General Jackson and his staff took a ride over the recently contested fields enroute to the rear. Having heard of Lieutenant Douglas' exciting and narrow escape, they were teasing him about his "big jump," the story of which he had related to them earlier. Coming near to the place where it occurred, Lieutenant Douglas persuaded the group to go a little out of their way to see the proof of it. The general consented and they rode over to the spot. After studying the area for a moment, Jackson turned in his saddle to the staff and said:

"Gentlemen, the evidence is conclusive—that—Douglas was very badly scared!"

Then, according to Douglas, Jackson, with what was almost a chuckle, ambled off to headquarters.

33/127

Come Again?

An artilleryman of Parker's Virginia Battery, Private Royal W. Figg, described himself as one of the "praying boys," meaning he was of the percentage of soldiers who had a religious nature. Nevertheless, Figg had little faith in those who claimed a piousness they did not have. He believed that most wartime or battle-field "conversions" did not last, and were for the moment only. He also found that some men he knew possessed great faith only when their god answered prayers; otherwise, they could be cowards or worse. Combining some of these elements, Figg wrote about an incident at the Battle of Second Manassas, August 30, 1862, involving a soldier he called "Boanerges," although that was not his real name.

Boanerges was the type of fellow, said Figg, who before the start of the war, proclaimed that the Southern army "would manure Virginia soil with Yankee car-casses." In reality however, in this, their first real battle of the war, Parker's Bat-tery saw that the Federals, instead of peaceably giving up their bodies freely for cheap fertilizer, came on in droves, in heavy lines of battle, and their demeanor was alarmingly belligerent.

Therefore, recalled Figg, this new and grave situation caused Boanerges to call up the "heavy artillery." He knelt behind the earthworks thrown up by the Rebels for defense, and began to pray with great enthusiasm, if not with total faith:

"O Lord, drive them back! O Lord, drive them back!"

Anxious for a speedy answer to his urgent plea, he partly rises and asks, "Boys, are they coming or going?"

"Coming!" was the alarming reply.

He again falls to prayer, and, if possible, with more energy than before, im-plores the "Lord" to "drive them back!" To his tremulous question, however, "Are they coming or going?" the awful answer still is, "Coming!" At last af-ter a third and most urgent storming of the "throne of grace," Boanerges is told that "the Yankees are going!"

With this news, his martial energies are aroused. He seems a very son of Mars as he springs upon the breastworks, defiantly exclaiming, "Come back here, you cowards! Come back here! We'll whip you!"

The enemy had been only demonstrating, and there was little or no fight-ing; but this experience convinced Boanerges, and others too, that his talents lay in another direction. He sought and obtained a chaplaincy.

24/69

Corn-federate Wisdom

In early September, just following the Battle of Second Manassas, General Lafayette McLaw's Division of Longstreet's Corps went into bivouac near Leesburg, Virginia. The men of his command had recently come through a time of meager rations, where even the foraging in the countryside had been poor, and they were hungry. Fortunately, it was the season of the year when corn was ripe in the fields, but it was no help to the troops. The general had issued orders to his soldiers not to touch an ear of corn in any of the Southern civilians' lush fields.

Soon however, one farmer near McLaw's camps noticed that raids were being conducted on his crop. He asked for help and the general placed guards nearby to protect the eatable property. These sentries were told to arrest every man coming out of the field with corn, and bring the pillager and his plunder to headquarters:

It was not long until the "pirouters" [pirates] began to appear, under guard, in the presence of the irate commander, and as each one, with his arm load of corn, halted before him, the General opened on him like this: "Where did you get that corn?" and the culprit would begin: "Why General, I had nothing to eat for three days, and I didn't know when the wagons would come"—but there the General stopped him with the order: "Put it down there on the ground and go join your command immediately!"

This movement, being many times repeated, caused quite a large pile of corn to grow up in front of the General's quarters, and in answer to the savage-toned query—"What are you going to do with that corn?" every one made the same excuse of "hungry," and "wagons not come up," etc., and in each case the order was, "throw it down on that pile and go join your command immediately." Finally, one "gray jacket," who had "caught on" to the manner and form of the proceedings, was brought up and accosted fiercely, with the question: "What are you going to do with that corn?" "Why sir," said the culprit, briskly, "I'm going to throw it down on that pile thar, and go and join my command immejitly, I am!" The General broke down, the guards roared, and the cute Reb slid out "immejitly," but the quartermaster took charge of the corn and issued it to the men, who made it last until the wagons came up with rations.

22/116

Mother's Sweet Milk

During the Antietam Campaign in early September 1862, cannoneer Edward A. Moore, of the Rockbridge Artillery, was given permission to visit Frederick, Maryland, by his battery commander, Captain William T. Poague.

While strolling through the pretty streets of that fair city early one evening, he met a comrade, Joseph F. Shaner. Private Shaner, after a long walk, had finally arrived in the town, but was too late to enjoy the opportunity all soldiers dream about: a day of leave from the army, spent in a prosperous metropolis, teeming with all the good things of life. Moore, seeing Joe's "woeful dejection," and because his friend was tired, hungry, and overheated from exertion, offered Shaner a taste of whisky which he had acquired in his rambles that day.

"It's just what I need," was Shaner's reply, and before Moore could get the canteen strap over his shoulder, Joe had dropped to the ground, placing one knee on the curbstone, and had turned the canteen upside down to his mouth, oblivious of anyone passing by.

In retelling the story, Captain Poague explained that while Joe was down on the ground guzzling at the canteen spout, a couple of civilians came strolling by. One looked over, and spotting the two soldiers, called out:

"Just look at that old cow and calf."

8/135 & 19/42

Run Doc, Run!

The day before the Battle of Antietam, on September 16, 1862, the 1st Georgia Regulars were in position near the town of Sharpsburg, Maryland, where they came under a very sharp artillery fire from the Yankee lines. The sergeant-major of the regiment, William Andrews, called the pounding "one of the hottest artillery duels I ever witnessed." During that severe bombardment, Andrews said he noted several "extremes of bravery and cowardice," in the conduct of his men. One of the cases of cowardice that was exhibited caused much amusement. It involved Surgeon William R. Bickers, and was described by the sergeant:

The fire was so distressingly hot that the doctor was completely scared out of his wits and made a break to run. Some of the boys called to him, "Run here doctor, here is a safe place," and he wheeled and made for that part of the line. By the time he would get there a shell would explode close to him. Back where he came from, another fellow would call to him to run there, that he had a safe place, and away he would go to find a shell when he got there. The whole line was enjoying the poor fellow's antics and when a shell would explode near enough to him to almost lift him off his feet, [they] would nearly bust their throats cheering at him. Poor fellow, he did not succeed in finding a safe place on the line, and made a dash for a small swamp to our right and rear. Then the boys rolled over and yelled themselves hoarse.

Following the Antietam campaign, reports were filed on the battle, as was the usual procedure. One day, remembered Sergeant Andrews, Captain Lewis H. Kenan was making out a list of casualties inflicted on the regiment while in Maryland. Lieutenant Gus Rutherford came up, and in his dry way, told Captain Kenan that while writing his report, "he must not forget to mention that the gallant assistant surgeon of the 1st Georgia Regulars, Dr. Bickers, had his horse killed under him while gallantly leading the wounded to the rear."

"The lieutenant," said Andrews, "seemed to think that the gallantry of the doctor ought to go on record."

46/76, 88

Tongue Tarred

Anyone familiar with the Battle of Sharpsburg, Maryland will have read of the exploits of the 1st Texas Infantry of General Wofford's Brigade, Hood's Division. On that day, September 17, they fought like tigers, and in doing so, lost 186 men, including 45 killed in action.

Another loss occurred to the Texans that bloody day—their beautiful and cherished flag was captured by the Federals. It was an honorable incident, of course, because the color-bearer was shot down at his post doing his duty. In the words of Joseph Polley, a soldier of the 1st, "the enemy was pressing the regiment too vigorously for its members to attend to any duty but shooting."

Several days following the battle, the "colorless" 1st Texas was marching along a Maryland road, when it happened to pass another regiment, the 6th North Carolina Infantry, a famous unit from the old "Tarheel State." One would-be wag of the 1st Texas, with "wit," but no thought and little discretion, sang out to the 6th: "Halloa, fellers! have you a good supply of tar on your heels this morning?"

"Yes," answered a long, lean Carolina man pleasantly. "[A]nd it's a real pity you'uns didn't come over and borrow a little the other day; it mout have saved that flag o' your'n."

20/85

'Bama Bound

Captain Silas T. Grisamore was quartermaster of the 18th Louisiana Infantry when it went into camp for a period of weeks in the fall of 1862 near Pollard, Alabama. During those enjoyable autumn days, the men of the regiment purchased and perused the Mobile newspapers almost daily. In particular, the soldiers took notice of a column in one of the papers entitled: "See What Alabama Has Done." In it were accounts of praiseworthy events, or of brave Alabama military units going to the front to fight for their state and the Confederacy.

The Louisiana boys found this to be very "cute," and the title of the column quickly became a "by-word" with the 18th. So anytime something having to do with Alabama was noted, the men would call out, "See what Alabama has done!" For instance, if a soldier came into camp with a gopher he had caught to eat, he would walk through the bivouac, holding up the creature, saying, "see what Alabama has done."

While at Pollard, Captain Grisamore, in his position as regimental quartermaster, received a shipment of clothing for the 18th Louisiana, some of which had been sewed by the kind-hearted women of Alabama. The only problem which arose from this gesture, was that portions of the uniforms were too large. The reason being, the Louisianians were very small in build, as Frenchmen tend to be, while the clothing had been sewn by the local women for their larger bodied, mountaineer husbands, brothers, and sons. The military jackets on the other hand, were factory made, and had been constructed through state contracts. They were just the opposite in size, and generally so small as not to fit a ten-year-old boy.

One warm, comfortable day, after the men had completed drill, the camp became quiet as the soldiers all returned to their tents to sleep, read, or lounge in the shade of the trees. But for his relaxation, a devilish little Frenchman named Private J.H. Masson, had a different idea, as here described by Silas Grisamore:

[Masson] put on one of the biggest pair of pants he could find and by rolling up a yard of each leg succeeded in getting his feet clear; then he put on a shirt that reached to his knees and a jacket that would not button by six inches and extending barely half way to his waist; then he put on a small kepi with the visor down behind. And thus equipped, he issued out of his tent and with both arms extending into the air ran all around the camps yelling at every jump, "See what Alabama has done, see what Alabama has done."

Whilst the sleepy boys, being thus summarily aroused from their dreams, raised a whoop the like of which never was heard in those woods before.

52/97

Ride 'em Cowboy!

Following the Sharpsburg Campaign of September 1862, the Army of Northern Virginia army went into camp near Bunker Hill, Virginia. One evening, after midnight, Lee's cavalry chief, General J.E.B. Stuart, rode into the headquarters of General Stonewall Jackson's Corps. With the general was Major John Pelham, commander of Stuart's "Horse Artillery." As the hour was late, and everyone had gone to bed, Stuart, who was a close friend of Stonewall's, went directly to Jackson's tent. Pelham found his own berth nearby, with a staff officer, Lieutenant Henry Douglas.

General Jackson was sound asleep; Stuart, exhausted, threw himself down by the general's side, taking off nothing but his saber. And since Lieutenant Douglas heard the rest of the story first-hand, we shall let him tell it:

As the night became chilly, so did [Stuart], and unconsciously he began to take possession of blankets and [even] got between the sheets.... [In the early morn, Stuart, finding himself so entangled and still fully dressed, got up and went outside.] After a while, when a lot of us were standing by a blazing log-fire before the General's tent, he came out for his ablutions. "Good morning, General Jackson," said Stuart, "how are you?"

Old Jack passed his hands through his thin and uncombed hair and then in tones as nearly comic as he could muster he said, "General Stuart, I'm always glad to see you here. You might select better hours sometimes, but I'm always glad to have you. But, General"—as he stooped and rubbed himself along the legs—"you must not get into bed with your boots and spurs on and ride me around like a cavalry horse all night!"

33/196

Borrowed, Mostly

After the Battle of Antietam, the Union Army of the Potomac remained for a time in camps around Sharpsburg, Maryland to rest and resupply its needs. During this period, the army was visited by President Abraham Lincoln, and a grand review was planned in honor of his presence.

In among the throng of guests at the review were some of Robert E. Lee's Confederate veterans. They consisted mostly of wounded prisoners captured in the late engagement who were still recuperating in Federal hospitals nearby. One of those Rebel soldiers was a member of Company C, 15th Virginia Infantry, described as "a tall, stout, robust fellow; a dare-devil, rollicking chap, who gloried in a fight." He was known to his comrades by the nickname of "Beauregard." This fellow and the other Southern captives had been carried out to the review on stretchers and then placed on cots, all presumably invited in order to impress them with the might and power of the Yankee nation.

President Lincoln stood nearby, and during the review watched the troops while mounted on a large, impressive horse, wearing a very tall silk hat, making in all, as one eyewitness affirmed, a towering picture of a "gaunt, raw-boned angular citizen in ill-fitting clothes and awkward manners."

C. HAZARD

Part of the military parade was devoted to the artillery, and several hundred field guns passed in front of Mr. Lincoln and the other visitors in an imposing and powerful spectacle. When the show was over, the president rode up to the Confederates, drew rein near "Beauregard," who had caught his eye, and addressed him thusly: "Now, Johnnie, tell me, what do you think of our artillery? Honest now, a square opinion?"

"Well, Mr. President, I will tell you: it surely does look fine, and there's lots of it, too. In our army we haven't got so much, but it looks just like yours. On nearly all the limber chests there's the letters "U.S." same as yours."

"This retort, courteous and so straight from the shoulder, greatly pleased Mr. Lincoln, who never failed to see and enjoy a good joke, no matter at whose expense, [or] whose undoing. He rode on, trying in vain to suppress laughter."

2/15/121 & 33/171

Oh, Nellie!

One could make the argument that this next story could be included in either a Confederate or Union book of humor, and it probably does belong better in the latter. But since the anecdote also concerns a Southerner, General Ambrose P. Hill, it can fit in here.

It was common knowledge to many, both before and during the war, that in his youth, Ambrose Hill had fallen in love with Mary Ellen Marcy, daughter of Randolph B. Marcy, who became a Union general in late 1861. Unfortunately, another good man, George B. McClellan, was also her suitor. Both Hill and McClellan had been cadets together at West Point, and each served in the Mexican War. Ultimately "Nellie," as Mary Ellen was called, married McClellan in 1860.

When war came to the country in April 1861, both men went their separate ways, one to the North, the other South. But the rumor continued that Hill had never gotten over the loss of Mary Ellen to George B, and this belief was kept alive by a goodly number of Rebs and Yanks. Then it so happened that some Federal soldiers began to notice that in McClellan's campaigns around Richmond, and even at Sharpsburg, General Hill's Confederate troops were often in the forefront of battle. And when in this particular position, Hill's "Light Division" tended to attack either their front, flank, or rear, and especially early in the morning. Obviously, after a while, the Yankees under "Little Mac" grew tired of that sort of treatment. They also began to attribute their problems with Hill to his spite and vengeance toward McClellan for winning "Miss Nellie."

"Early one gloomy morning," as one scenario was said to unfold, "before the sun had appeared, there were shots of artillery and rattle of musketry which told of a spirited attack. Hill was at it again. The long roll was beaten, there was commotion and confusion and a rush to arms, in the midst of which one hardened old [Union] veteran unrolled himself from his blanket and in an inimitable tone of weariness and disgust, cried out, 'My God, Nelly, why didn't you marry him!'"

33/178

The Dude

Company E, of the 2nd Texas Cavalry, had on its organizational rolls a Marylander named William Simpson, whose pre-war occupation was that of professional gambler. But "Sim," as he was called by his friends, always described himself in a more positive manner, as "a dealer in pasteboard and ivory."

In the late summer, or early fall of 1862, Private Simpson was given a furlough, which he spent very productivly in San Antonio. Sim returned to camp two days late, although just in time for payday. And to make amends, Simpson promised his captain that from hereafter he would be a "good soldier."

Soon the regiment was mustered for paycall, and everyone was present in ranks ready to march off, except Private "Sim." The men waited patiently for a while, but finally the captain, tiring of the hold up, sent a trooper to retrieve the wayward soldier. Private Clarence Key later described in detail the arrival of their comrade:

> ...[P]resently Sim came with colossal self-assurance. He was ridiculously gotten up: dressed in a black frock coat (Prince Albert), black satin waistcoat, black doeskin trousers, and patent leather Oxford tie shoes, boiled starched shirt, standing collar, black satin cravat, and a diamond stick pin. He was armed with a brand-new Enfield rifle, a new Colt forty-five, a new, shining cartridge box and belt. He came out smiling blandly and not in the least abashed at finding that we had been left behind by the regiment because of his delay. When he took his place in the ranks, the captain called to him sharply: "Simpson!"
>
> "Sir?" said he.
>
> "What do you mean by coming on parade in those ridiculous duds, sir?"
>
> Sim looked himself over with a very self-satisfied glance and said: "I was told to put on the best I had for muster, Cap'n, and I did so."
>
> "Didn't you get a gray cloth [jacket] and a hat the other day like the other men?"
>
> "Why, yes," said Sim, smiling amiably. "Yes, Cap'n ..., I got one all right, thank you, sir."
>
> "Very well, then, go and put them on at once."
>
> "Yes, Cap'n," said Sim. "I'll do it with pleasure. Certainly, Cap'n... I'll do it with pleasure."

2/19/19

The Drill Master

To any soldier, a leave of absence was about the best thing army life had to offer. Sergeant C.W. Short of the 17th Louisiana, remembered how one of the non-commissioned officers of his regiment was turned down for such a leave, but in an interesting and comical manner. His unit was then manning the defenses of Vicksburg, Mississippi in the late fall of 1862, about six months before the great siege took place in the following year.

"A young sergeant...greatly desired a furlough, and lacked only the approval of General Stephen D. Lee, then commanding the forces at Vicksburg. He sought the superior officer, who refused his request politely but firmly, saying: 'I have orders to furlough no one. It is expected that the enemy will bring every possible means to bear upon this place at an early date, and therefore we cannot spare any of our good soldiers; they should be drilling every day.' 'But,' argued the sergeant, 'that does not apply to me for I am well drilled.' 'I shall try you,' said the General. 'Take position! About, face! Forward, march!'"

"The sergeant saw the joke before he got back to camp."

2/7/103

The Nose Knows Not

When an artillery unit deploys its guns and goes into "battery," or into a firing position, the drivers turn the limbers and caissons a little to the rear and attempt to park in a relatively safe location. Since the ammunition chests carried by these vehicles are vulnerable to enemy fire, it is advantageous to be removed from the battle line by even a hundred yards or so. However, due to the common practice of overshooting a target, the rear areas often became as dangerous as the front. Therefore, the drivers keeping watch over the horse teams and battery vehicles, took every opportunity possible for self preservation. Some even went so far as to scoop out little depressions in the ground to lay their bodies prone where the projectiles would have a more difficult time "seeking them out."

The Battle of Fredericksburg, Virginia, on December 13, 1862, was especially remembered by surviving Confederate veterans as an artillery "hell." Captain William T. Poague's "Rockbridge Artillery" came under a heavy bombardment after 1 p.m. that day, with Poague stating that, "[s]uch a tempest of shot and shell, I never have witnessed anywhere during the war."

While observing the effects of the Yankee guns, the captain noticed an artillery driver named John Connor holding his lead horses by a strap, as he lay face down on the earth, with his head up close to a small sapling. Poague couldn't resist a comment:

"Hello, John, that's a mighty small protection for your head."

Connor replied: "Yes, Captain, but if there was a ground squirrel's hole near by I think I could get into it."

In the same area lay another soldier who was stretched out behind a good sized old tree stump, with his nose within about a foot from a pile of filth, likely fresh horse manure. A comrade "seeing the situation and coveting that stump for himself exclaimed, 'look at that stuff near your face.' 'Pshaw, go away! it smells sweet as a rose,' the soldier replied and still stuck to his stump."

19/58

The Truth Now!

The night of December 28-29, 1862, was cold and a light rain was falling in the vicinity of Murfreesboro, Tennessee. Confederate and Union forces under Braxton Bragg and William Rosecrans, faced each other on what would become known as the Stones River battlefield.

After a late supper near midnight, the pickets of the 9th Kentucky Infantry, C.S.A., were suddenly driven in by the Yankees, who came rushing in on the Kentuckians in the pitch dark. A volley of musketry drove them back, but it also brought forth a volley of curses from one of the 9th's members, Michael McClarey. He had been out on the picket line and was trying his best to return with an injured man when the shots from his own men pierced the darkness, and threw him into an angry frame of mind. McClarey was a very brave man, but being shot down by his own side was not something he looked on with favor.

One of the soldiers present that evening was John W. Green, who finished the account in these, his own words:

His comrade was wounded & to bring him home through a corn field where the stalks had not been cut down & take care of his gun at the same time was a difficult task, but with his comrade on his back Mike came swearing at us most vociferously. "Sure are you trying to kill your own men?" But his di[s]gust was immense when upon laying his wounded friend down he discovered that a second ball had gone through his head & killed him, where upon he remarked, "I thought you said it was your leg you were shot in."

28/65

In and Out

During one of the fiercest battles fought in the Western Theater, which could have been at Murfreesboro, a celebrated Tennessee infantry regiment found itself in a position that any veteran would concede presented a valid excuse to make a quick "retrograde movement." These Tennesseans, while driving back a Yankee line, suddenly came upon a half dozen enemy batteries, which opened fire at short range with shell, shot and canister. At the same instant, several Union regiments added intense and close musketry to the surprise.

The Confederates, as brave as they were, found it best to fall back to a ridge two hundred yards in the rear. This meant leaving behind many of their comrades on the ground, killed and wounded, as they sought shelter to regroup and reform their ranks.

At this juncture, a noted Mississippi regiment came upon the scene. Its gallant colonel, "anxious for the fray, and not altogether apprised of the nature of the situation," shouted to the Tennesseans: "Make way *there*, and let Mississippi *in*."

The "way" was promptly made and the newly arrived Rebels rushed unhesitatingly at the foe. Soon they reached the point where the Yankees had slaughtered the Tennesseans, and a similar deadly greeting was given them.

"Earth and air seemed lighted with the fires and resonant with the roar of the infernal regions," and they reeled back as their predecessors had done. Seeing them return, the Tennesseans rose as one, and yelled, "Make way *here*, and let Mississippi *out!*"

1/1/64

Mr. Lipscomb's Target

The Confederacy began conscripting men into the ranks of its armies in early 1862. The "luster" of being in the military had worn off, and it was becoming harder and harder to entice men to enlist. Under the conscription law however, was a government policy in effect which allowed impressed civilians to "dodge the draft." This loophole, for a time, made it legal for inducted men to hire a substitute to go into the army for them.

In Company E of the 1st Louisiana Cavalry were two privates who had come into the regiment as substitutes for draftees. They were both well advanced in years. One of them was Sidney J. Gee who had enlisted for a Mr. Lipscomb back home in Louisiana, and the other was Jerry Allspaugh who had joined in place of another fellow.

During the several days of the Battle of Murfreesboro, the 1st Louisiana was engaged in some minor aspects of the overall fighting. In one segment of the action, the troopers found themselves under a heavy fire, with bullets pouring through the regiment like hail. While this skirmish was in full swing, someone in Company E called out to the two aged substitutes, who were both hard at work shooting back at the Yanks like everyone else:

"Look out, old gentlemen, you are going to get hurt here the first thing you know."

"Oh, that don't make any difference," answered one of the ancient soldiers, Private Gee. "It won't be me, it will be Mr. Lipscomb that will be killed."

41/173

Do I Have To?

During the winter of 1862-1863 the 45th Illinois Infantry was posted in Memphis, Tennessee, acting as the provost guard, or what was the military police force of the Yankee-occupied Southern city. The colonel of the regiment, Melanchthon

Smith, was the acting provost marshall. Any citizen in sympathy with the Confederate government was required to swear to and sign an oath that they would not aid or abet the Rebel army in any way, particularly if they wished to travel out of Union held territory.

One day a cultivated young woman from a prominent family in Memphis, Mary Erwin, applied to Colonel Smith for a pass so that she might send clothing to several friends then in the Confederate army. Smith instructed Erwin that she would have to take the oath. She answered him by saying that she was surprised that he would advise her to swear. The colonel replied that she must swear before she could get the pass. She begged to be excused. He was adamant. Mary then appealed to other Federal officers present in the office. She asked them to witness that she was compelled to swear to obtain the desired pass. Mary Erwin then raised her right hand, and said with emphasis: "God damn the Yankees." She got the pass.   2/2/369

1863

How Low Can You Go?

It was a very cold second day of January 1863, and the Battle of Murfreesboro had been in progress for almost three days. Captain William W. Carnes, commanding a Tennessee battery in Cheatham's Division, was given instructions not to fire at any Federal artillery which may be directed against his position. He was supposed to remain quiet, and keep his guns "masked," or hidden, so as to be prepared to repel any infantry assault which might be aimed at the Confederate lines.

Occasionally, some Union battery would "stir the pot," and lob a few rounds into the Southern ranks. With orders to keep silent, Carnes' artillerymen sought all available shelter to protect themselves from the deadly missiles coming toward them.

Right after one of these periodic shellings had ended, Captain Carnes was signaled by his lieutenant to glance in the direction of a certain veteran driver of one of the horse teams named Andrew J. Matthews. Private Matthews was removing his blanket from one of the horses and spreading it upon the ground, which was still wet from a recent rain.

The lieutenant remarked: "Matthews is going to make himself as comfortable as possible, even under fire. He is a cool fellow; look at him now."

The soldier in question had just laid down full length on the blanket, and with a laugh, stated that he was tired of getting up and down during the bombardments, and was fixing himself to stay for the rest of the performance. Just then, another cannonade began and lasted several minutes, causing the Rebs to "lay low." When the danger had passed, Matthews jumped up, shook out his blanket, and replaced it in its former location. Seeing this, the lieutenant called out: "What's the matter, Matthews; is your blanket getting too wet on the ground?" The soldier shook his head slowly and then, with a serio-comic expression on his face, answered: "Oh no, sir; I was not considering the good of the blanket, but of myself. When those things are flying over my head like that I want to be as close to the ground as possible, and just a minute ago that blanket seemed a foot and a half thick."

This is reminiscent of the artilleryman in Parker's Virginia Battery, Tom Kirtley, who in a similar circumstance at Fredericksburg stated emphatically: "I don't want nothin' under me, not even a sheet of paper; but if there be paper, I don't want no writin' on it."

24/65 & 2/1/264

Dogfaced

The 5th Alabama Battalion of General Henry Heth's Division, Ambrose P. Hill's Third Corps, spent part of the winter of 1862-1863 in camp near Orange Court House, Virginia. On one occasion during this period, General Robert E. Lee ordered a grand review of his army. Sergeant William F. Fulton of the Fifth was present that day, and recollected a curious and comical moment during the review:

> *[The] entire command was paraded in a large open plain.... As the different commands assumed their positions and the entire formation was adjusted, it looked grand and imposing. Mrs. A.P. Hill, [Kitty M. "Dolly" McClung], the wife of our Gen. Hill, accompanied by several ladies, drove up in an army ambulance drawn by four horses. They stopped immediately in the rear of our command, where Mrs. Hill could get a commanding view of the magnificent scene. We soon ascertained that the wife of our loved commander was in the ambulance and all had a desire to see her. It was whispered along the line that some officer should request her to grant us that favor; and Capt. Archibald N. Porter, of Co. B, a rather pompous young officer from Calhoun County, Ala., assumed the role. With his cap in one hand and his sword in the other he approached the ambulance, and making his best bow and a military salute with his sword, he said, "The Fifth Alabama Battalion wishes to see Mrs. A.P. Hill. Will you be so kind as to show yourself at the door?" This may have been altogether out of place—I do not know about that—[but] it actually occurred. And Mrs. Hill, in a flash, poked a little dog out of the window remarking as she did so, "This is the general's favorite."*
>
> *We laughed at Capt. Porter's expense, but failed to see the general's wife.*

37/60

Spurred On

During the late winter of 1862-1863, several two-gun detachments, or "sections" of Captain William T. Poague's "Rockbridge Artillery," were moved back and forth from various duty positions and/or encampments as their service was required. The winter was a hard one, and the men and animals of these sections had suffered greatly from light rations and fodder, plus the constant exposure to the elements. By spring, the horses, after having served in such barren regions of Virginia, were in very poor condition.

One of these detachments, for a time, was bivouacked twelve miles from Port Royal at Jack's Hill overlooking Port Tobacco Bay, and had undergone an especially hard time. Finally after several weeks orders arrived which required the section to return to Port Royal, a more prosperous and healthy region. The men, excited about the prospects of better food and quarters, packed their equipment, harnessed the teams, and moved out. But the horses, due to their broken-down condition, could barely pull the limbered guns and caissons, which were axle deep and held tight by the frozen mud of the dreadful winter roads.

One of the drivers was a tall and long-limbed Virginian named Jim Tomlinson. He was mounted on one of the animals trying in vain, with voice and spur, to urge his exhausted team to do its best. Coming upon the scene, and seeing Jim's situation, was the comic of the battery, 44-year-old Irishman Tom Martin, and he immediately called out: "Pull up your frog-legs, Tomlin, if you want to find the baste. Your heels are just a-spurrin' one another a foot below his belly!"

8/168

Parlez Vous "Croak"?

A few of the regiments formed in the central and southern parishes of the State of Louisiana contained a large number of French speaking individuals. Confederate units from other states posted near these foreign-sounding soldiers, were often amazed at their unique language and the speed in which the Frenchmen were able to speak in their rapid-fire and strange "lingo."

During late 1862 and in the early months of 1863, various Southern military organizations took turns fortifying and garrisoning Port Hudson, Louisiana. This site on the Mississippi, like Vicksburg, had been prepared to resist the Union army and navy's free navigation of that important river. Eventually the longest siege of the Civil War occurred at Port Hudson, where the bastion surrendered to Federal forces on July 9, 1863, five days after the capitulation of Vicksburg.

Earlier however, on the night of March 14, and prior to the start of the siege in May, a Yankee fleet under Admiral David G. Farragut, attempted to pass up river by steaming by the heavily fortified gun positions of Port Hudson. The ensuing bombardment was terrific and sublime. Scores of large caliber artillery pieces fired by the Confederate shore batteries and the Federal gunboats made the darkness seem like day, and nature's thunder sounded insignificant by comparison.

One of the Confederate regiments called out that evening to prepare for a possible land assault was the 30th Louisiana, which was made up of French-speaking men. Ordered to the earthworks alongside the Louisianians, was an English-speaking unit. A soldier present with this latter regiment made the following observation:

> *While we were standing in line, in the darkness, close to the quarters of the Thirtieth Louisiana, we noticed that the frogs in the numerous ponds seemed much excited, and were croaking incessantly in a kind of low continuous chatter. One of the boys listened a moment, trying to make out what it meant. At length he announced the explanation: "Boys, these frogs have been camped so long by the Thirtieth Louisiana that they have learned to talk French."*

2/1/308

Very Profound

The 4th Massachusetts Infantry, at one point in its nine-months military service, and prior to the investment of Port Hudson, spent some days camped at Baton Rouge, the capital of the state of Louisiana. While visiting the city, Private James F. Dargan of Company D, met an ex-Rebel soldier who said his name was Lazarus Billings. Billings had supposedly been in one of General P.G.T. Beauregard's regiments during the Battle of Shiloh, and was then out of the army and back home selling produce. Dargan struck up a conversation with the Southerner, and came away with a little poem Billings had composed. It was entitled, *Du Profundis.*

I would not be a generaul
  with gold braid on my hat;
It takes too sharp a feller, and
  I'm rather slow for that.
I would not be a curlonel,
  with stars upon my kote,
Because they never mentions him
  In Borygod's repote.
I would not be an officer
  In any companiee;
Responsibility's too grate
  Entirely for me.
I would not be a solgier
  And having to be drilled
Because he never gets his dues
  Untill he's gone and killed.
I think I'd ruther stay at home,
  where I can sleep at night;
And leave the Klory to Providence,
  And them what wants to fight.

16/np

A Weighty Question

Sometime during General Basil Duke's raid into Kentucky, and just after the fight at Danville on March 24, '63 the 1st Louisiana Cavalry found itself on another long, tiring march. In among the column was Second Lieutenant Howell Carter of Company E. As he was riding slowly along, he happened to take note of one of the regimental servants, a slave named George, who was carrying a cased violin strapped to his saddle. Carter knew that the violin had been taken out of one of the wagons captured from the Yankees as a prize of war. But he also felt that since the raid had been extremely hard on the horses, he should say something to the servant. George, on the other hand, was very fond of the instrument, and intended to take it home to Louisiana when the opportunity presented itself. Lieutenant Carter made his decision, looked toward George, and instructed: "Throw that box away, George, you cannot weight that horse down in such a manner."

"You won't care about me keeping it if the weight is not on the horse will you?"

"Of course not," Carter replied, and with that George threw the violin upon his shoulder, saying as he did so: "I'll pack it myself."

41/73

Hats Off!

One of the most important pieces of uniform clothing that a soldier required, was a good, sturdy hat or cap. Living life predominantly "out of doors," made a headpiece essential to the Confederate of the 1860s. And since the government could never keep up with the demand for official military headgear, the average Reb had to look to his own methods for covering the "ole noggin."

A private in the 7th Virginia Infantry named David Johnston, recalled how one of his companions of Company D, James H. Gardner, procured a hat in March of 1863.

While situated in camp near Petersburg, Virginia many men in the regiment would often go into the city on leave, some with permission, and others without. One day, Private Gardner returned from "French leave," and was found to be wearing a fine looking hat, instead of the old, dingy dirty cap he had worn when he started off to town. When he was asked how he obtained such an excellent new headpiece, Gardner replied:

"I swapped with a fellow—but he wasn't there!"

Private Gardner had certainly found a clever way to steal a hat, but for uniqueness, the "Texicans" of General John Hood's Division put the rest of the Confederate Army to shame.

In early May of the same year, the 7th Virginia was camped for a short while at Chester Station on the Richmond and Petersburg Railroad, about ten miles directly south of Richmond. Hood's Texas and Arkansas Brigade was in bivouac just across the railroad tracks from the 7th. Upon the approach of a train, the

Texans would place rows of musket percussion caps on top of the iron rails, and then hide out in the brush near the tracks, and await the results of their handiwork. As the train rolled in, it crushed the small brass caps, causing them to explode. The effect was that of a sharp "pop" or "crack," similar to the sound of a small "cap gun" or firecracker. Naturally when the caps fired off, curious passengers would look out of the windows, many even sticking their heads through the openings to ascertain the cause of the popping. But upon drawing their heads back into the coach, the innocent and naive folk found themselves hatless. The soldiers had rushed out of hiding and stripped them clean.

This was a hard lesson, but one that worked again as each new train pulled into the station.

23/185 & 43/70

Gunboat Fever

As a member of General John B. Hood's Texas/Arkansas Brigade, Private William C. "Bill" Calhoun of the 4th Texas was famous far and wide as one of the most interesting characters in that composite of many unusual individuals.

In April 1863, the brigade was serving southeast of Petersburg, Virginia, and within sight of a fleet of Union gunboats on the James River near Suffolk. One day General Hood, then a division commander, halted near the camp of the 4th to speak to Colonel John Key on some business. While so engaged Hood noticed Bill Calhoun nearby, and knowing his personality, decided to have some "sport" with him. So in a voice loud enough to be heard by the entire regiment, the general said to Key:

> "Detail an officer and twenty five of your best men, Colonel, and order them to report to me at once at my quarters. I have set my heart on one of those gunboats down on the river, and I know that [number of] men of the Fourth can easily get it for me."
>
> Bill heard and accepted the challenge. Stepping to the side of Hood's horse and laying one hand on the animal's neck, while [with] the other he touched the brim of his hat in respectful salute to the rider, [and] he said: "Now look ah-here, General, if you've just got to have a gunboat, whether or no, speak out like a man and the Fourth Texas will buy you one, but we don't propose to fool with any of them down yonder in the river. They say the darned things are loaded, and, besides, there's only a few of us fellers can swim."

20/113

Little Stonewall

The Confederate soldier was no exception when it came to enjoying animals, whether it was in camp, on the march, or even in battle. Pets were common in the service, provided much amusement to the men, and are fondly recalled in their letters, diaries, and memoirs. There were pet birds, raccoons, squirrels, chickens, geese, goats, cats, and of course, the most favored, dogs.

One dog must take a front seat when we study the menagerie of regimental or battery mascots on record. His name was "Stonewall Jackson," and he was adopted by the Richmond Howitzers in 1862. Described by a "Howitzer" as a "Welsh fice," the pup was "very small, but beautifully formed, gleaming white in color, with a few spots of jet black, his hair fine and short, and lying close and smooth." But "Stonewall" was most remembered for his heroic behavior in battle. "A born warrior" they called him. "When our guns were in action he was always careening wildly about them, and in any pause of their hoarse thunders the shrill treble of his tiny bark was always to be heard."

Sergeant Van McCreery in particular, took a special interest in "Stonewall," and became his "master, teacher, patron and friend...." While many of the "Howitzers" taught him tricks, it was Sergeant McCreery who made him a legend in the army. And Private Robert Stiles here chronicles his fame for future generations:

> *Van taught Stonewall to attend roll-call, and to sit up on his haunches, next to him, on the advanced rank of non-commissioned officers, and he made a little pipe for him, which Stonewall would hold between his teeth. Then when the orderly sergeant, before beginning the roll, called "Pipes out!" Van would stoop and slip Stonewall's pipe from his mouth to his left paw, which would then instantly drop to his side with the other, and the little corporal would stand, or sit, stiffly and staunchly in the position of a soldier, eyes front, until the company was dismissed.*

It appears, though, that the "little corporal" became too popular, and too irresistible for his own good. He was "dognapped" from his unit and recovered several times by the Howitzers. The culprits were the Louisianians in General Harry T. Hays' Brigade, they, "having the ungovernable passion of the French soldier for pets."

At last, according to Stiles, their mascot was taken and hidden for good, "to the deep regret, not to say grief, of every man in the battery."

38/171

Bland Humor

The 7th South Carolina Infantry was fortunate to have as one of its field officers, an "ideal soldier," Lieutenant Colonel Elbert Bland, who never received promotion to full colonel, but led the 7th from September 1862, to his death at Chickamauga in September 1863.

Bland was described as a fighter "par excellence," with a gift of inspiring in his men the lofty courage that he himself, possessed. In appearance, "his form was faultless—tall, erect, and well developed, his eyes penetrating rather than piercing, his voice strong and commanding." To those qualities was added a noble, generous nature, plus coolness and bravery under fire that almost ran to rashness.

Bland's men idolized him for one more reason. Under his guise of sternness ran a streak of gentle humor, which to a soldier, made him the ultimate comrade and leader.

The following story illustrates that "lighter side" of the good colonel, and shows the direction his humor could take.

Just after the Battle of Chancellorsville in early May 1863, Colonel Bland was ordered to carry a message, under a flag of truce, to General Joseph Hooker, who was in command of the recently defeated Union Army of the Potomac camped across the Rappahannock. When he reached the enemy's side of the river, he was met by Yankee officers and a crowd of curious onlookers who wanted to catch a glimpse of a Rebel soldier, and to see why he had come over.

Being then a lieutenant colonel in the Southern army, Bland had two stars stitched to his coat collar to show that rank. In the Confederate service one to three bars on the collar indicated a second lieutenant to captain, while one to three stars meant the rank was major to colonel. The story continues:

> One of the younger Federal officers made some remark about Bland's stars and said, "I can't understand your confederate ranks; some officers have bars and some stars. I see you have two stars; are you a Brigadier General?"
>
> "No, sir," said Bland, straightening himself up to his full height; "but I ought to be. If I was in your army I would have been a Major General, and in command of your army."
>
> Then with a merry chuckle [he] added, "Perhaps then you would not have gotten such a damned bad whipping at Chancellorsville."

At that, everyone in the crowd had a hearty laugh!

54/282

Munford's Magic

Prior to the Siege of Vicksburg, as General U.S. Grant was making his push toward that fortress city, several battles were fought against the Confederates led by General John C. Pemberton. Eventually, after losing these engagements, the Rebels were forced to retreat into the Vicksburg fortifications, a move which doomed Pemberton's army into a surrender on July 4, 1863. One of the actions in this campaign, and the largest, was that of Champion's Hill, or Baker's Creek as the South called it, which occurred on May 16, 1863.

On that day of fighting Southern morale was low, as Grant's forces seemed unstoppable. The Union army had been victorious in other earlier battles, and now with many good officers and men shot down, the Rebel cavalry line near Baker's Creek was becoming unhinged, as a strong enemy column pressed the rear-guard steadily backward. Furthermore the shaky troopers were not helped any by the shells and bullets which were flying around, as thick as a swarm of angry hornets, tearing up the ground, shredding tree limbs, and in general making the locality a mad, terrifying, and very unsafe place to be. It required great composure for a man to stand his post.

According to eyewitnesses, there was a deadly silence on the part of the Rebel cavalrymen of Adams' Brigade. No one knew what the next minute would bring, but still the rear-guard held its ground. Suddenly, a man lost his nerve! This increased the intensity of the moment. That soldier, who was mounted on a good horse, went dashing to the rear. As he flew by, he hollered out: "I can't hold my horse." Just then, Munford Bacon, of the 1st Mississippi Cavalry, saw the bolting horseman, and heard his weak explanation for leaving the line. Bacon raised up in his stirrups and yelled out: "Boys, I will give $1,000 for one of them horses you can't hold."

This created a laugh and a yell, which steadied the men and slowed the enemy, allowing the Confederate cavalry to secure a better position. Munford Bacon's quick wit, it was said, helped prevent disaster at Baker's Creek.

2/3/270

Artiste de' Rump

General J. E. B. Stuart was another colorful and interesting character in Confederate service. He was known also for the unusual and entertaining people he associated with, and who made his personal staff so enjoyable to be around. One such person was Captain Justus Scheibert, II, a stoutly built, Prussian army engineer who had been sent to America to observe the military movements of the Army of Northern Virginia.

In late May 1863, Stuart's Cavalry Division was in bivouac near Orange Court House, Virginia. Stuart had recently enticed Scheibert away from Robert E. Lee's headquarters, so his presence might enliven Stuart's own staff with his simplicity of character and odd, amusing personality.

One day Captain Scheibert was invited to the village to visit with Charlotte Wickham, the wife of General William H. F. Lee, one of Stuart's brigade commanders. Mrs. Lee was fond of art, and as Scheibert had some skill in painting, he was asked to come over to the boarding house where she was staying to touch up one of her sketches. The piece in question was an oil sketch of a small-size female head that Charlotte Lee had just completed.

On that occasion, Scheibert was wearing a very short cavalry style jacket and white trousers, "in which his fat person looked as if it had been melted and poured in, so tight was the fit." After working on the figure, Scheibert laid the canvas, still moist with its sticky paint, on a chair. Meanwhile the captain became engaged in an animated conversation with his hostess. At one point as he moved about and gesticulated in his normal eager and excited way, he completed his sentence, and plopped himself down on the nearest seat, which happened to contain her recently completed artwork. This went unobserved by both parties, for the day was hot and the blinds had been partially closed.

When it was time to leave, Mrs. Lee thanked Scheibert and told him to please keep the picture as a souvenir of their pleasant acquaintance. When he looked around to pick it up, he exclaimed: "Bless my soul! I laid it down on one of the chairs, but I don't see it now." Believing it had fallen down under a nearby piano, Scheibert got down on his hands and knees to find it. In doing so, Charlotte Lee saw the wet portrait stuck firmly to his large rear end. "Here it is" she cried, screaming with laughter, as she peeled the unfortunate canvas from the broad seat of the captain's white trousers. This gesture however, had left the lovely face of the female, somewhat blurred, transferred most conspicuously upon his abundant derriere.

Scheibert then quickly backed out from under the piano, and without stopping to retrieve his hat, cane, or gloves, he bolted off for Stuart's camp, "waving his arms wildly and roaring like a bull with laughter."

26/207

Mexican Standoff

In the opening chapter of this book, we looked at instances of comedic abuse heaped upon civilians and soldiers foolish enough to enter the world of the infantryman, outfitted in unusual or "dandified" hats, boots, uniforms, mustaches or hairstyles. Here, written by Allen C. Redwood of the 55th Virginia, is one of

"Don't turn that thing loose, hit's dangerous."

those encounters, a classic in its own right. Redwood, on this occasion, was acting in the capacity of a mounted orderly, and the gist of the story centers around
a pair of fancy Mexican spurs he was wearing, the kind with "jinglebobs" and
huge, sharp pointed rowels measuring several inches in diameter. In other words,
Redwood had inadvertently set himself up for his own "roasting:"

> *Thus appointed, the writer happened to be detained one day upon the road
> by an infantry column at a halt, and immediately became the focal point of a
> cross-fire of remarks, called forth by his unlucky gaffs. The blocking of the
> road by the stacked muskets and recumbent men forbade all hope of escape,
> and there was nothing for it but to face the situation with as good a grace as
> might be. "Mister, how old does ye hev ter git afore they comes out that long
> on ye?" "Don't them things keep ye 'wake o' nights?" were among the ob-
> servations vouchsafed. With an assumption of the gravest interest, one fellow—
> the self-constituted fugleman of the regiment...—inquired if they were "Yankee"
> spurs, and being answered in the negative, rejoined, "Well, ye've tuk a load
> off'n my mind, fur I reely wouldn't like ter fight nobody with sich things on
> 'em." Another exclaimed, "This hyar must be the hoss-artillery don't ye see
> hit's got wheels?" At last, in the vain hope of ridding myself of an interest
> which had become oppressive, I unbuckled one spur and held it aloft, in full
> view of all. This proceeding called forth the remonstrance:*
>
> *"Mister, fur the Lord's sake, don't turn that thing loose; thar's a chance o'
> people in this hyar road, an' hit's dangerous!"*

Hanging On

When General John Hood's Division of the Army of Northern Virginia entered Maryland in late June 1863, after crossing the Potomac River on its march north into Pennsylvania, it halted near Williamsport. There, a rare occurrence took place. The division was issued a ration of whiskey, something not often done in the Confederate army. One of the members of Company F, 4th Texas Infantry provides us with the details of what happened next:

> *There was only about a gill [1/2 pint] to the man, but as the temperance fellows gave their shares to friends, the quantity available was amply sufficient to put fully half the brigade not only in a boisterously good humor, but in such physical condition that the breadth of the road over which they marched that evening was more of an obstacle to rapid progress than its length. At an early hour John Brantley, of my company, became so exhausted by his latitudinarian tendencies as to prefer riding to walking, and perceiving that Colonel [John C. G.] Key was in an excellently good-natured condition, took advantage of a momentary halt to approach that gallant officer, and, slapping him familiarly on the leg, remark, "Say, Kunnel! I'm jes' plum' broke down; can't you walk some an' lemme ride a while?" Bending forward over his horse's neck and grasping the pommel of his saddle with both hands to steady himself, the old Colonel looked pityingly down at Brantley and, between hiccoughs, replied, "I'd do it in a minute, ole feller, damned if I wouldn't, but I'm tired as hell myself, ah-sittin' up here an' ah-hol'in' on."*

20/121

The Conversion

During the Gettysburg Campaign, while bivouacked in the same Williamsport, Maryland location as related in the above story, another incident occurred which helped to enliven some of the Texans of Lee's army.

One evening, Company K of the 5th Texas Infantry was detailed on guard duty at General Hood's headquarters near a large farmhouse. About midnight, some men brought in a young country fellow, who was as naive and "green" as they come. He had been caught trying to "bushwack" some Confederate soldiers with an old single barrel shot-gun. Hood ordered Company K to guard the man until morning, when he would be turned over to the provost marshal of the division.

The Texans saw an opportunity for some fun, and they immediately began to chide and harass the frightened boy with a fearful story. He was told that General Hood always shot "bushwackers," and the only thing that would save him was a membership in the same church as the general. When asked about his religion, the youth answered that he was a Dunkard. The serious-looking Rebels then expressed mock sympathy for the "bushwacker." The Texans explained that it was too bad he was not a "Cambellite" like Hood, as this would probably save his life, for the general was never known to have had a follower of his faith shot. By this time the poor fellow was scared within an inch of his life, and believed wholeheartedly that he was doomed to death in the morning. Finally, although he hated to convert, if it would save his life, the boy said he might consider it.

The soldiers kept him worked up to a fever pitch all night, and in the morning, after breakfast, General Hood walked over to where the prisoner stood under arrest.

"You're a bushwacker, are you?" asked the general. "Yes, Sir" was the reply.

And all the while, the Texans were winking at him and silently encouraging him to tell Hood his new religion.

As Hood talked, the young man was trembling like an aspen leaf, always watching the guards, and trying to figure a place to get in the fact that he was now a Cambellite. Eventually, after giving the frightened fellow a healthy lecture about the seriousness of his act, General Hood told the sergeant of the guard to turn him over to the provost marshal. At that moment, the poor lad looked like he would sink to the earth.

"With a death glare in his eyes and the most intense fear marked upon his countenance...[h]e looked around..., and then raising his hands he gave a most unearthly shriek, and squealed out in a sort of half shriek and half sob, 'I-I-I'm a Cambellite.'"

At this, the Texans let out a yell. Hood looked around, unaware of the joke. As the bushwacker was led away saying, "I'm gone. I know that he means to have me shot," and he began to weep most piteously.

Naturally, of course, he was treated as a prisoner of war, and no harm came to him at all.

34/108 & 55/235

Dead Man Walking

In the Battle of Gettysburg fought July 1-3, 1863, Lieutenant George H. Mills commanded Company G of the 16th North Carolina Infantry, part of General Alfred Scales' Brigade, and General William Pender's Division. His memory of the first day of combat, written down years later, was brief and to the point. But the incident described here was surely enough to cause Mills laughter long into the future, although his humor was probably cut short that day, for he was wounded soon after it happened:

> ...[A]bout 2 P.M. [we] came in sight of Gettysburg and were soon moved to the right in a lane with a wheatfield in our front. Tearing down the fence, the order came "forward, march," and the 16th, with Pender's Division, moved forward at quickstep pressing to the left, and after marching about a mile in line of battle through the ripe wheat, we came up to the artillery posted on a bluff, and firing rapidly. Passing in front of the guns, we lay down and watched the fight going on for half an hour, Heth's division being on the line in our front. While lying here the guns in our rear kept firing over us and some [Yankee] guns on the opposite side replying, several

of our men were hit by fragments of shells. One Captain was struck and his head was cut and scratched in several places. He jumped up and started to the rear hollowing at every jump, "I'm dead, I'm dead."

The Colonel of his Regiment called two stretcher men and told them to "go and take that dead man off—if you can catch him."

50/36

Flopped, Fleeced, and Fled

The early afternoon of July 3, 1863, just south of Gettysburg, was not, by any means, a pleasant place to be. For at that time over two hundred cannons were belching smoke, fire, and iron at each other across the intervening fields, woods, and ridges of a section of Cumberland Township, Adams County, Pennsylvania.

While Union and Confederate artillerymen made the very earth shake with fury, and filled the atmosphere with the terrible sounds of flying metal and exploding gunpowder, the lowly infantrymen of both armies hugged the ground and waited out the deadly barrage. For soon it would be their turn to fight, so during the long bombardment the men sought shelter wherever they could find it.

While these violent scenes were being acted out, George Bernard of Company E, 12th Virginia, was privy to a curious episode that occurred nearby, told to him by his friend, Pat Drinkard.

During the height of the cannonade, when the shells and balls were screeching furiously overhead, and the detonations of some of the projectiles were producing fear and consternation in the prone ranks around him, Drinkard, like others, took cover behind one of the immense oak trees in the vicinity.

Not too long afterwards Pat was joined by a nervous Georgian, who, coming from the front lines, ran up and plopped down next to him behind the tree. Now the fire became even more intense, and the unwelcome visitor was not content to merely lie at Drinkard's side. Fearing he was too exposed, the interloper drew closer and closer to Pat, until he eventually mounted himself onto Drinkard's back, like a tick to a dog. There he remained, said Pat, until a lull in the tempest gave the Georgian an opportunity to escape further to the rear.

Drinkard, feeling somewhat abused by the whole incident, was later even more indignant. Pat soon discovered that the uninvited guest, even in his terror, had had the presence of mind to slip his hand into the Virginians haversack and steal a handful of bread, which constituted all of Drinkard's reserve rations.

5/16

Portable Heat

In September 1863, most of General James Longstreet's Corps was sent by General Lee to reinforce General Braxton Bragg's Army of Tennessee, which was then in position near Ringgold, Georgia. Since a majority of the trip was made by rail, and the officers' horses, ambulances, artillery, etc. traveled by the highways, there was a period of time before and during the Battle of Chickamauga, that the men carried only their basic weapons and equipment.

It was only natural then, when seen in this condition by the veterans of the Army of Tennessee, that Longstreet's men were "ribbed" for marching so light—no horses, camp baggage, cannons, supply vehicles, and the like. This also meant, of course, that regimental, brigade, and division officers were forced to march on foot alongside their commands. One day, General Henry L. "Rock" Benning was met by a regiment of Alabama soldiers, walking at the head of his Georgia brigade, carrying only an ax.

Trying to be "cute," one character asked Benning why he did not carry a blanket, as the early fall weather in Northern Georgia was becoming cooler. The general replied promptly, "that an ax kept him warmer than two blankets."

47/134

Come Sup With Us

Anyone reading through personal accounts left behind by Confederate soldiers, will often find references to the various chaplains who served with the army's many regiments and brigades. Some of the recollections are positive, but there are other quotations attesting to the poor quality of these religious characters, especially the "Go thouest" variety of minister, versus the "Come hither" type. In other words, there were enough of the "do what I say, not what I do" kind to be noticeable. The following is an example of that unpopular style of preacher.

The 1st Tennessee Infantry certainly never forgot a run-in with a bold and gallant chaplain, a certified "L.L.D.," from Nashville, who rode an old "string-haltered" horse alongside General George E. Maney's Brigade on its advance into the Battle of Chickamauga, Georgia, in September 1863. As the brigade marched closer and closer toward the fighting, the holy man exhorted the soldiers to be brave, to aim low, and to "kill the Yankees as if they were wild beasts."

A Tennessean present in the ranks that day should be allowed to continue the account:

> He was eloquent and patriotic. He stated that if he only had a gun he too would go along as a private soldier. You could hear his voice echo and re-echo over the hills. He had worked up his patriotism to a pitch of genuine bravery and daring that I had never seen exhibited, when fluff, fluff, fluff, fluff, FLUFF, FLUFF—A whir, and a BOOM! and a shell screams through the air. The reverend L.L.D. stops to listen, like an old sow when she hears the wind, and says, "Remember, boys, that he who is killed will sup tonight in Paradise." Some soldier [then] hallooed at the top of his voice, "Well, parson, you come along and take supper with us!" Boom! whir! a bomb burst, and the parson at that moment put spurs to his horse and was seen to limber to the rear, and almost every soldier yelled out, "The parson isn't hungry, and never eats supper."

45/114

Old Jube's Jibe

General Jubal A. Early was unquestionably at the top of a list of the most interesting Southern officers to participate in the American Civil War. He was, as General Lee put it, "one of my bad old men." But Early was also loyal, had great courage and a fine native intellect; he was self-reliant and resourceful, and of course, was known, and somewhat feared throughout the army for his caustic, biting tongue. "Old Jube" was also the only man who dared to swear in the presence of General Lee. Early, all in all, was somewhat of a privileged person in Confederate circles, for as it was once said, he was "saucy to everybody."

Before the war, Early had been an intense pro-Unionist, but when Lincoln called for troops to put down "the rebellion," he became completely "Rebelized," and stayed that way until his death.

During the Virginia Secession Convention in April 1861, Jubal Early voted against secession, and often had serious disagreements with the Honorable Jeremiah Morton, who was as extreme a Secessionist as Early was a Unionist. Morton was very fond of talking about "our rights in the territories," meaning of course, the right of Southerners to own slaves there, and for the power of a territory to chose to be a free or slave state.

When hostilities began, Morton, who was a very rich landowner, did not enter the army, most likely due to his age, which may have disqualified him for military service. His handsome estate "Morton Hall," however, was situated in an area of Virginia where dozens of battles and skirmishes were eventually fought.

It seems that on one occasion, later in the war, Mr. Morton narrowly escaped capture by a Yankee raiding party. He was obliged to mount his horse that day and hasten to safety. And as it so happened, the vanguard of the force sent to stop this Union incursion was led by General Early himself.

Riding at the head of the column, Early spotted Morton, "coming in hot haste, digging his spurs into the horse's flanks." The general quickly ordered a line of his men to bar the road and intercept Morton's headlong progress. And as the frightened and flying figure galloped past, "Old Jube" playfully called out:

"Hold on, Morton! Are you going for our rights in the Territories?"

38/189 & 40/100

Easy Does It, Mister

It was during the Battle of Chickamauga, Georgia on September 19, 1863, that Private Adam C. Anderson made history in his regiment, the 15th Texas Cavalry. When dismounted, Anderson, a member of Wise County's Company B, was tall "out of the saddle" at 6 foot, 4 inches, and as brave as any man in Cleburne's Division, Army of Tennessee.

On that bloody day in Georgia, the 15th moved forward against the enemy and soon came under heavy fire. This brought the Texas cavalrymen to a halt near where General James Longstreet, who was commanding an entire corps, sat on his horse observing the action. The men did not recognize Longstreet; he was new to the Army of Tennessee, having just come southwest from Virginia where he had served under General Lee. That day Longstreet would have been hard to identify as a general in any event, for he was wearing a common "backwoods" hunting-shirt, with no insignia of rank, and an old slouch hat.

Meanwhile back on the firing line, Private "Ad" Anderson had fought so hard that eventually his gun got fouled with burnt powder and "choked," as the saying went, and would not take a cartridge. He then turned away, and began slowly and leisurely to walk to a safe place to clean his gun. As Anderson was heading rearward, General Longstreet spotted him and commented: "Hello, my good fellow, you are not going to leave us, are you?"

"Ad" stopped, looked up at him, and countered: "See here, you damned old hunting-shirt snoozer, do you know who you are talking to?"

Longstreet laughed heartily at the reply, and then explained who he was. Soon he and Private "A" were on good terms and parted as friends.

Needless to say, "Ad" was the man of the hour that day!

49/157

Catching Hell

The major of the 8th South Carolina Infantry, Eli T. Stackhouse, was known as one of the most stubborn fighters in that regiment. He was also near 40, a long-time farmer, and a strict Methodist of the purest kind, said to be a "churchman of the straightest sect." An officer who knew Stackhouse thoroughly, claimed he always said what he meant, probably never had an evil thought, was blunt in speech and manners, forever sincere, and used chaste language; well, with the possible exception of this one occasion.

During the Battle of Chickamauga Stackhouse was in command of the right wing of the 8th. On one occasion during the fight, the Federals made a furious assault on a portion of his line. The major could see them coming. He rose to his knees from the ground where the men were in firing positions, and called out to his troops: "There they are, boys, give them hell!" Then in an undertone he would say, "May God, forgive me for that!" Still the Yankees did not yield, and again and again he shouted louder and louder, "Boys, give it to them; give them hell!" with his usual undertone, "May God, forgive me for that," etc. etc.

Soon, however, instead of slowing down, the Yanks began closing in on his right and center, and his left was about to give way. The brave old soldier could stand it no longer. Springing again to his feet, his tall form towering above all around him, he shouted at the top of his voice, "Give them hell, give them hell, I tell you boys, give them hell, God damn their souls."

"The Eight," remarked one of the officers in Kershaw's Brigade, "must have given them what was wanting, or they received it somewhere, for after this outburst [the Yankees] scampered back behind [a] ridge."

54/281

Give 'em "You know...!"

The following anecdote is a lot like the previous tale, but this time around we focus on a much bigger fish, Confederate Lieutenant General Leonidas Polk. Polk was born in North Carolina, and studied to become an Episcopal minister after his graduation from West Point in 1827. By the outbreak of the Civil War, he was already the "Missionary Bishop of the South West." But rather than stay with his church, Polk chose to join the Southern army, and was appointed major-general on June 25, 1861. Two years and three months later, at the Battle of Chickamauga, the bishop, then a lieutenant general, was commanding a corps in the Army of Tennessee. It was there that our story of Polk unfolds.

The day was September 20, 1863, and an attack by Longstreet's Corps was in full swing. General Polk rode up to General Benjamin F. Cheatham and ordered him to move his division forward to support Longstreet. General Cheatham, to give his men encouragement, and a good send-off into the attack, called out: "Forward boys, and give 'em hell." General Polk also wanted to encourage the troops with a little verbal support, but due to his position in the clergy, did not use profanity. So he settled for, "Do as General Cheatham says, boys!"

45/118 & 49/218

Hooded Threat

Private William Calhoun of the 4th Texas Infantry, like most of his comrades in General John B. Hood's old brigade, loved and respected the legendary leader, who by 1863, had made his reputation as a hard fighting division commander in the First Corps of the Army of Northern Virginia.

But that loyalty could be pushed a little too far. After all, when Hood was promoted brigadier-general, the Texas Brigade had raised a great sum of money to purchase one of the finest horses in their state to present to the general. Then there had been his Gettysburg wound.... And recently, at the Battle of Chickamauga, General Hood had lost his leg to enemy fire. So again the brigade came forth with its love and generosity. It began to collect cash from the rank and file members, in order to outfit John Hood in one of the best artificial limbs available on the market.

The day finally arrived when Bill Calhoun was called upon for his share of the gift. An eyewitness was there and recalled the moment. Bill "fished it slowly out of the depths of his pocket, then removed a quid of tobacco from his mouth, drew a long, solemn breath, and remarked: 'I ain't got a stingy bone in my body, an' you fellers all know it; but twined around every fiber of my mental caliber is a never-dying sperrit of rigid and uncompromising economy, and I want old Hood to know that hereafter he must curb his impetuosity and stay further in the rear. He orter know he can't do any good close to the Yankees; and if he keeps on like he's been er doin,' it'll bust this old brigade er buyin' horses and legs for him.'"

2/5/218

Hammer Time

The 9th Kentucky was one of the regiments of a brigade in Breckinridge's Division, Second Corps, Army of Tennessee. Following the Battle of Chickamauga in late September 1863, the Kentucky Brigade was ordered to Tyners Station on the Western & Atlantic Railroad south of Chattanooga to guard commissary and quartermaster stores, and to help protect the rear of the army. Upon arrival the men quickly built huts to protect themselves, as the October weather was turning cool and damp, and their clothing was in rough shape after a summer of hard campaigning.

While on duty at Tyners, the soldiers of the 9th were often in contact with a group of Alabama troops who shared the varied responsibilities there. The Alabamians, nicknamed "Yellowhammers" by the rest of the army, due to the color of their uniforms, often received large wooden boxes from their home folks containing food, clothing, and other delicacies. It was difficult for the other troops stationed at Tyners not to feel tempted by the large assortment of treasures these boxes held.

One night the temptation became too great, and two Kentuckians slipped through the Alabama sentries and stole a large box which they believed was filled with gourmet delights. The next problem was, "how to get it passed the 'Yellowhammers.'" Fortunately one of the Alabamians was coming off a tour of duty, and was enticed and bribed to let the box slip past, so he could share in its bounty. The big crate was carried down to the Kentucky camp deep in the woods and opened, where all present began to divide the contents.

Kentuckian Johnny Green described the ensuing scene:

> It proved to be a rich haul indeed, three hams, delicious pickels & preserves, nice warm wollen socks, two coats, a pair of shoes, & various other good things. The Ky boys each took a coat & as the shoes just fit Alabama they said, "Here Yellowhammer you may have these shoes."
>
> The socks & other things were pretty fairly divided but finally they came to a letter at the bottom of the box & Kentucky said, "Yellowhammer as we sort of got you in the division of coats & socks you may have the letter."
>
> He threw some fresh wood on the fire to make a good light to read the letter by while the other two stretched themselves to rest awhile. Alabama soon grew serious & he turned to the end of the letter to read the name when he exclaimed, "Look here boys, dern my fool skin! This box is from my mother, sent to me. Now look here, Youens aint going to keep my things is you?"

In the end some compromise was made, but a deal was a deal, contended the Kentucky duo. "Alabama" must not have been too pleased at the outcome, for on the next night he procured another box, and with the assistance of a friend carried off the stolen prize. However when the lid was opened, the two Yellowhammers found a dead soldier inside, packed and ready to be shipped home for burial!

No one has said, but this last episode may have put a dent in the box stealing business.   28/106

Mistaken Identity

The Battle of Wauhatchee, Tennessee was fought during the night of October 27-28, 1863, between troops of General James Longstreet's Corps, and a portion of General Oliver O. Howard's Federal Corps, and General John Geary's Division. In the confusion of that dark battlefield, some Confederates at one place were flanked and driven out of their position. One of these units was the 15th Alabama Infantry.

Of all the company commanders in that regiment, Captain William N. Richardson stood out as a very eccentric man. He was an educated and well-to-do farmer, who often amused his comrades with the curious and strange peculiarities of his personality. The colonel of the 15th Alabama, William C. Oates, once repeated a story concerning Richardson in the fight at Wauhatchee.

When the Yankees flanked the Alabamians on the left as stated above, they got dangerously close to the Rebel rear. Oates' men retreated, and tried to get away as fast as they could with as little loss as possible. As the 15th broke and ran, Oates remembered it "as a very mixed state of affairs:"

> *The eccentric captain, whose organ of locality was so deficient that he had but little idea of places or directions, got lost from his company in the woods, and hearing the voices of men went to them, and walking up among them remarked, "Well, boys, that was a devil of a fright we got a while ago." One placed his hand upon Richardson's shoulder and said, "You are my prisoner." The Captain inquired, "What command is this?" A response came in the nasal twang of the down-easter, "Eighty-second new York." [sic] The Captain just then awoke to a realization of his condition. He said, "Look here, gentlemen, I am most egregiously mistaken. I thought this was the Fifteenth Alabama. By heavens! this ought not to count."*

They laughed and sent him to a military prison, where he remained until nearly the close of the war.

Richardson was the same fellow who in November 1862, had become somewhat inebriated while the regiment was crossing the Blue Ridge at Miles' Gap. While on that march he was quoted as saying: "[T]his is the largest war I was ever caught out in and therefore if I take a drink or two and don't get drunk it is all right."

Later that day, as Captain Richardson staggered along the roadway in the rear of the 15th, (after stumbling down the entire mountainside), he was heard to mutter: "The drunken man falleth by the wayside, but the sober man passeth over the mountains safely and sleepeth in the valley beyond."

48/165, 283

The Bridge on Raccoon Mountain

The Battle of Wauhatchie, Tennessee, as we know, took place on October 28-29, 1863, but the men of the 4th Texas always called it by the name of Raccoon Mountain. It was the only time in their history, stated a member, that the 4th "stampeded like a herd of frightened cattle."

Raccoon and Lookout Mountains are separated by Lookout Creek, and between the creek and Raccoon Mountain there are several high, flat-topped parallel ridges; Raccoon itself, was steep and heavily wooded.

On the night of the 28th, General Joseph Hooker's Federal corps was camped in the vicinity of Raccoon Mountain. It was proposed to General James Longstreet that General John B. Hood's Division could march to the west side of Lookout, and by a night attack, capture "Fighting Joe's" Yankee force. Yes, and all things are easier said then done, for from that moment on nothing went as planned.

After a tiring march, the 4th Texas, as part of Hood's force, finally lay down for a rest on the crest of one of the flat ridges near Raccoon. They were ignorant of the fact that the main body of the enemy was camped in a wide and deep depression below two of the ridges, and between the Texans and Raccoon Mountain. The Confederates had barely dropped off to sleep when a gunshot awakened both armies. All at once the stillness of the night erupted like a volcano blowing its top.

Scouts were sent out, and the 4th found it was quite alone, basically lost, and about to be attacked by the aforementioned Union troops. With no hope of support, and hearing the enemy laboriously struggling up the ridge toward them, the little band of Texans did what they had never done before, they ran like scared sheep! The Yanks came at them with a rush, a yell, and firing their muskets. The Rebels tumbled and skipped and slid down the steep slope, rushing pell-mell to safety through the black, thick woods. Men fell, screamed, and ran headlong into trees; it was every man for himself.

At the bottom of the ridge, testified one of the Texans, there "was a ditch-like drain that marked the line where descent of one hill ended and ascent of the other began." It was here, he claimed, that an incident occurred which would forever be remembered in the regiment.

An exhausted litter-bearer by the name of Thomas E. Dennis, a six-footer with a huge belly, at the moment the ditch was reached, tripped, and tumbled in. The fall knocked his breath out, and he had strength only to wriggle out of the drain onto his back; his head was propped up on one side of the ditch, his feet on the other. Just then, as Dennis was becoming somewhat comfortable, along came Bill Calhoun plunging down the hill. He saw the recumbent man's body, and taking it for a log, "made a tremendous leap, and landed his foremost and heaviest foot right in the middle of Dennis' expansive corporosity." The sudden compression brought a grunt and a howl of agony, and Tom Dennis cried out, "For the Lord Almighty's sake, man, don't make a bridge of a fellow!"

Bill was naturally startled, but he never lost his presence of mind, and shouted right back, "'Lie still, old fellow, lie still! The whole regiment's got to cross yet, and you'll never have such another chance to serve your beloved country,' as he continued his flight with a speed but little abated by the rising ground before him."

And forever after, Private Tom Dennis was known as "Old Pontoon."

2/5/106 & 6/219 & 2/26/20

The Pampered Louse

No one should attempt a collection of Confederate humor without including an account of the old-time "grayback" louse, or *Pediculus Vestimenti*. These tiny unforgiving creatures were so well known by all Civil War soldiers, as to have become "legends in their own time." One infantryman summed up their ever-presence by declaring simply, that each body louse should have had stamped on his or her back: "I.F.W.", or "In for the war."

There are hundreds of excellent primary sources that make mention of these devilish insects. One of my favorites which chronicles the "comings and goings" of this "depraved little pest," was recorded by Captain William "Buck" Walton, Company B, 21st Texas Cavalry. Here is his excerpted version:

I found that many of the men had been familiar with these varments a long time—and become accustomed to their presence. So much so, that it was part of their amusement to catch the big ones and bet on their fighting qualities. It is true that the grown bug, when taken from the bodies of different men—and placed close together, will rush at one another like bull dogs, and fight to the death—or until one, being whipped and wounded, will scramble out of reach of his adversary. This I saw tested one day when a number of my men [were] gathered together, watching very intently such a fight. They had two "big fellows" on the top of a hat, smoothed out. There was considerable excitement, and the men had their Confederate money—and [were] flourishing it, as I have seen men do at a horserace. I walked up to see what was the matter, and saw the whole fight. The bugs were just coming together—and they

certainly were mad. The gladiators unarmed save with their natural weapons [were] joined in conflict. It was a battle royal. They stood up on their hind feet. They closed in grapple and would roll over & over. They seemed never to weary. The battle lasted five or six minutes. The blood was very perceptible on each one. Their legs were broken and [there were] wounds on their bodies—to such an extent that they were maimed—and neither could run from the other. The two warriors could do nothing, but lay on the field of battle and lingering die.

Actually some of the men would not molest a very fine specimen—but let him grow and fatten on his own blood until he thought he had the most robust "gladiator" in camp-and then would draw him forth privately and try his powers on a smaller specimen—that he would borrow or steal, from another man. When he had tested him and made him bold by whipping smaller fellows—his owner would challenge the field—having the champion—& offer to bet on him, like he owned a press that threw off Confederate money as wanted. Sometimes they made a run with their pampered louse, and became very flush. And then some man would find a still [more] pampered one, & win all his money. Many are the ways that idle soldiers find to amuse themselves—but [I] really think this was one of most unique ways that I saw in the army. I called on two boys for two of their champion "gladiators"— for a special purpose. They cheerfully gave them, and I took them & in a letter to my Captain's wife, Mrs. Wm. Rust, at Burnet, Texas, enclosed them to her—to see what we could do in the army. They were received—and proved of the right gender—& before she was aware of it, she was in possession of a large & flourishing colony, which caused much washing and disenfectants before she could get rid of it.

17/73 & 88/23

Easy Does It

North Carolina soldiers had a reputation in the Rebel army for taking things slower and more relaxed than even the easiest-going Southerner. Their walk, speech, and other movements were often spoken of as being "as slow as molasses poured in winter." This did not, of course, affect the fact that "Tarheels" fought well, and eventually lost more men in battle than any other Confederate state.

This relaxed nature, however, belied a subtle wit, which is apparent in the account which follows.

Zebulon B. Vance, who was elected governor of North Carolina in 1862, journeyed to the armies in the field periodically in order to bolster the spirits of his men. Having been a soldier, (colonel of the 26th regiment), Vance felt it his duty to see to the morale of his state troops whenever possible.

While preparing for one of these excursions, the governor secured a horse for ease of transportation to the various and scattered commands he wanted to visit.

This horse was far from being a purebred. It was very lean, extremely slow moving, and altogether, a pretty sad looking mount.

One day as Vance was riding this skinny beast to his next destination, he spotted a soldier in the distance, plodding along possibly even slower than his own old horse. The governor, who always enjoyed the humor of any given situation, recognized instinctively that the man was a fellow "Tarheel." As the soldier began to edge himself off the road, Vance called to him in a kindly manner, "You needn't move, my good man; I won't run over you."

"I know you won't run over me," was the drawling response, as he eyed the old nag, "but I don't want to be gored to death by a pack of bones!"

24/213

We're Busted!

Colonel Elijah V. White commanded the 35th Virginia Cavalry Battalion, a unit which traveled light, and was known for its scouting and raiding activities. Being less of a typical "line" regiment, the men resisted every effort made to arm them with rifles, muskets, carbines, or sabers. They preferred to stick to their trusty revolvers. And try as he might, Colonel White had difficulty keeping his troopers supplied with these regular "long arms," because on raids or scouts the men always found ways to "lose" them.

Eventually, as is usually the case in these matters, army bureaucracy caught up with the battalion. In the late fall of 1863, General Robert E. Lee wrote to General Thomas L. Rosser, who commanded the "Laurel Brigade" under which the 35th fought. In the letter, Lee questioned why no ordnance reports had been received from Colonel White's Battalion, and asked Rosser to look into the matter. General Rosser replied that he had never been able to get an ordnance report from the 35th, and if General Lee could do so himself, he would be glad to see it.

This "challenge" soon brought a staff officer directly from Lee's headquarters to Colonel White's camp, with the mission to get a report "at once." After introducing himself to the colonel, the inspector explained his business. "Very well, sir," said White, "go ahead."

With the help of White's adjutant, the report was soon partially made out, until Lee's staff officer, reading from a paper which he held in his hand, questioned: "I see, colonel, that 340 guns have been issued to your command, what report do you make of them?"

Colonel White turned to his adjutant and asked how many guns were on hand. The reply was, "eighty, sir." "Well, said the officer, "how do you account for the 260?" At this question, the colonel seemed somewhat perplexed. But while he was studying the matter over, one of his young troopers, in a corner of the tent, interrupted: "Why, Colonel, ain't them the guns that busted in Western Virginia?"

"I goly, yaas;" said White, "they did bust; you sent us a lot of them drotted Richmond carbines, and they like to have killed all the men."

Before he left, Lee's inspector wrote down in his report: "260 guns bursted in Western Virginia," and took his departure, everything being finally accounted for.

30/158

Stout Work at Payne's Farm

The Mine Run Campaign was the last major contact between the Army of the Potomac and the Army of Northern Virginia for the year 1863. During that campaign, on November 27, there was a skirmish south of the Rapidan River known as Payne's Farm. One of the units involved was the 21st Virginia Infantry of General Edward Johnson's Division. In that engagement, a sergeant of the regiment, John H. Worsham, witnessed a sight rare in the annals of military engineering:

> *I will mention a gallant action which I saw here. Captain John C. Johnson of the 50th Virginia was a large and stout man of about fifty years of age. Thinking that some of his men were not doing as well as they ought, he walked out to the brow of [a] hill, lay down on its top—broadside to the enemy, and then called to some of his men to come up. If they were afraid, he said, they could use him as a breastwork. Several of them promptly accepted his challenge. They lay down behind him, rested their guns on him, and fired steadily from this position until the fight was over. I am happy to say that the gallant captain was not injured.*

42/118

A Gem from General Lee

During the wars of the 19th century, public perception of military events predictably followed what the citizenry read and understood from its local newspapers. Editors in those days had great power, as these influential publications were the only means by which most people could get national news. The stand or slant they took on an issue, might make or break generals and politicians.

General Robert E. Lee was one soldier who understood what public opinion could accomplish or destroy when stirred up by an aggressive newspaper editor. Although he himself fared pretty well at their hands, Lee knew of many occasions in both the North and South, where editorials had changed government policy, or caused the replacement of high-ranking officers who commanded major armies.

Supposedly, sometime after the Southern disaster at Missionary Ridge, Tennessee in November 1863, and the resignation of General Braxton Bragg, Lee, in a private conversation, was said to have made the following satirical remark to Confederate Senator Benjamin H. Hill of Georgia: "We made a great mistake in the beginning of our struggle, and I fear, in spite of all we can do, it will prove a fatal mistake."

"What mistake is that, General?" asked Mr. Hill.

"Why, sir, in the beginning we appointed all our *worst* generals to command our armies, and all our *best* generals to edit our newspapers. I have done the best I could in the field, and have not succeeded as I could wish. I am willing to yield my place to these *best* generals, and I will do my best for the cause editing a newspaper. Even as poor a soldier as I am can generally discover mistakes after it is all over, but if I could only induce these wise gentlemen who see them so clearly *beforehand* to communicate with me in advance, instead of waiting until the evil has come upon us, to let *me* know what *they* knew all the time, it would be far better for the country."

22/129

1864

Tiny Tots

Captain R.S. Williams' Kentucky Artillery Battery was one of the most unusual military units in the Southern army. Organized in 1862, it contained about 25 men and six small unique "Williams' breechloader guns," (no relation to the captain) which, according to one writer, fired one-pound projectiles. The battery was subsequently commanded by Captain James J. Schoolfield, and was attached to a Kentucky cavalry brigade until it was disbanded in 1864. Due to the size of its cannons, the men of the organization and its half-dozen little field pieces, were often the butt of jokes by any comically inclined Confederates who came in contact with them.

Because of their mobility, the tiny guns were sometimes borrowed by miscellaneous regiments and taken on raids made by individual officers. One such excursion was led by Lieutenant Colonel Thomas Johnson of the 2nd Kentucky Cavalry Battalion, Mounted Rifles, who pulled one of the Williams cannons along with him. During this foray, the breechloader was captured by a Union partisan band, which entered Johnson's camp at night and stole the gun away. (Years later the Yankee partisan chief admitted that it was like having an elephant along—once he snatched the piece, he did not quite know what to do with it!) And as one would expect, the incident of the capture was the cause of much amusement to both Rebs and Yanks alike.

Some months afterwards, while Williams' battery was bivouacked in western Virginia, Colonel Johnson happened to ride by one day. Spying the five remaining artillery pieces, he could not resist the impulse to say something clever and sarcastic. So he accosted John Fish, one of the cannoneers, and suggested: "You had better keep your eyes on those guns or some woman may slip into camp and carry them off."

Private Fish, who did not know the colonel by sight, replied: "Oh, we are not uneasy. The only man in the army who would permit such a thing is Old Tom Johnson, and he is not in command here."

7/103

Keep It Coming!

John N. Opie served in both the 5th Virginia Infantry and later in the 6th Virginia Cavalry. Opie was also a soldier who could not resist a good joke. Here is one he told which combined two favorite subjects of the Confederate enlisted man:

A field officer of a certain cavalry brigade invited the other field officers to dine with him. On the bill of fare was apple brandy, which flowed freely. After the jug had passed several times, an old colonel arose, with great gravity, and said, "Gentlemen, my regiment met the enemy yesterday and overcame him. We killed fifty, wounded a hundred, and captured two hundred and fifty prisoners."

Those present commended the Colonel for his successful encounter; and again the apple-jack was vigorously and repeatedly assailed. Again, up sprung the gallant Colonel. Said he, "I omitted to inform you of a terrible conflict my regiment had with the enemy yesterday. We killed five hundred, wounded a thousand, and captured fifteen hundred prisoners."

Again the Colonel was congratulated upon his splendid victory, and the brandy continued to flow freely, when, finally, the old Colonel, by this time loaded for buffalo, staggered to his feet and said, "Gentlemen, I neglected to tell you of the most terrific battle of the war. On yesterday my command encountered the enemy, and killed ten thousand of them, wounded twenty thousand, and captured twenty-five thousand prisoners of war."

Whereupon the host, who was also loaded to the hilt, sprang to his feet, seized the jug, and exclaimed, "Here, Colonel, for God's sake take another drink, and kill the whole Yankee army."

25/52

The Stoned Battery

Picket duty was an important aspect of soldiering, yet especially in the cold months when the troops were not campaigning, it could also be long, monotonous and boring. True, the very survival of an army might depend on its pickets giving early warning of an enemy attack, but to the men stationed at these lonely sentry-posts, it was tedious to the extreme. Therefore, anything that broke up the dreary hours of guard duty was looked forward to and encouraged.

One incident which helped to do just that, took place during a Virginia winter in the latter part of 1863. It was recorded by a Confederate staff officer, McHenry Howard, formerly of the 1st Maryland Infantry:

Once some North Carolinians,...usually a staid set of men, undertook to vary the monotony of picket life by a practical joke,...at Morton's Ford. At this point a strong reserve was maintained, which occupied a house or yard about six hundred feet back from the [river] crossing, while at the same distance from the north...bank the enemy had a like force at a house which seemed to be also the headquarters of some officer of rank. The North Carolinians had found a pair of immense wheels with a tongue attached, probably used for hauling timber, which at a distance looked not unlike a gun carriage, although it would have carried a piece of great caliber. Upon this they mounted a huge hollow log, and providing themselves with a rammer and some large round stones, they suddenly dashed out with it from the house half way to the river, wheeled into position and pointed it at the opposite house, rammed with loud words of command a stone into the log, and seemed about to knock the enemy's headquarters about their ears. For a time there was considerable commotion on the other side. The [Yankee] picket line hurriedly prepared for action and the house was speedily emptied, the inmates, or some of them, not standing in any order in going but making for the woods at once. The joke was presently appreciated and, with much laughter, the lines resumed their status.

12/256

Scared Shirtless

In the winter of 1863-1864, the 1st Louisiana Cavalry was a mere ghost of its former self. The regiment was, due to hard service, in such pitiful shape, that in late January it was ordered from its camp with the Army of Tennessee near Dalton, Georgia, back to Louisiana. There, the regiment would recruit new members, and then aid the state forces in breaking up the many annoying raids being conducted by Federal troops in east Louisiana.

Traveling home was long and tedious, but the troopers made the trip interesting and even fun. One of the enjoyments and benefits of the journey were the evenings. After the day's long march, the men would seek out private houses to obtain food and shelter as a break from their regular camp routines.

Private Jacques Heeny of Company D was one of the youngest who participated in these outings. But an incident on a cold winter night broke him of that pleasant pastime:

One evening [Heeny] rode up to a large two-story house and asked if he could stay all night. He was invited in, then went out to see that his horse was attended to, came back and was given supper. A little while after, the lady of the house said, "I suppose you are tired, so whenever you feel like going to bed just go up the stairs and you will find your room at the head of the steps. You will see a light in it."

Going up, he found rather a dim light and a man in the bed. He thought nothing of this though, for soldiers were often put in the same bed even if they had never seen each other. Just as he retired a young lady and gentleman walked in and took seats. Heeny with his elbow nudged his bed-fellow, but didn't dare speak—it was a novel situation and he wanted to see it out. The young fellow (after talking a while) said, "Jennie, I don't believe this old war is ever going to end; you have been putting me off so long, and why should we postpone our wedding any longer?" "Wait," she replied, "a little longer, say three or four months and if there is no prospect for peace then we will marry." A nudge from Heeny meant for his companion to listen. She had scarcely finished the sentence, though, when the young fellow threw his arms around her, and kissed her with the loudest kind of a "smack," saying "You dear little thing, give me a sweet kiss for that." Vigorous punches from Heeny were repeated, and the girl said, "Oh! John, you ought to be ashamed of yourself, kissing me that way when we are sitting up with a dead body."

Up rose Heeny with the sheet over him, and down those stairs precipitately fled that boy and girl. Heeny, actually putting on his clothes as he ran, was right behind them and to the stable he went and, catching his horse, never stopped until he reached camp.

What became of the boy and girl? was afterward asked him. "Oh, my God, I don't know, and don't care. You can bet I never went back to find out."

41/105

Too Little Too Late

By the end of 1863 the Confederate government could no longer back its currency with the value of gold. It was quickly becoming worthless, and the subject was already the brunt of many jokes by civilians and soldiers alike. The average Southern private was, by 1864, fighting for approximately 40 cents in gold per month; but of course, he was not receiving hard money, only 11 dollars in paper, when and if he was even paid.

Captain Henry K. Douglas illustrated this sad state of affairs with some notes he kept on his financial situation in March 1864. The exchange rate was then 16 to 1, and Douglas, while on leave, had just paid $30 per day for board at The Spotswood Hotel in Richmond.

Furthermore, he declared, "it cost a friend $300 to give half a dozen of us a night supper at an eatinghouse, and a little later I have [listed] $9.75 (why not $10.00?) for two mint juleps, $1,500 for a uniform, and was offered $5,800 for a horse worth, perhaps, $250."

To illuminate further the drastic money problems of the South, Captain Douglas repeated this little tale: "About this time a Confederate cavalryman, being offered $5,000 for a somewhat seedy-looking steed, proudly reined up his bony Bucephalus and exclaimed, 'Five thousand dollars for this horse! Why, I gave a thousand dollars this morning for currying him!'"

33/272

Clowning Around

Sometime prior to the Battle of the Wilderness, Virginia, fought May 5-6, 1864, Colonel Charles Marshall, of Robert E. Lee's staff, purchased a "parti-colored horse" in a small country town. No one knew the history of the animal, and, as good horses were scarce in the Confederacy just then, Marshall probably asked few questions at the sale.

During the aforementioned battle, the colonel happened to be riding through an old field where there were numerous large tree stumps still standing among a new growth of scrubby pines. As he was making his way between the stumps, Confederate infantry nearby commenced firing toward the enemy. At the sound, Marshall noticed that his horse began to caper about in a queer fashion. Seeing one of the biggest tree stumps, the animal placed his fore feet thereon and started to move around the stump in a waltzing fashion. The hotter and more intense the gunfire, the more he would dance.

On the scene was an observer, who explained the novel behavior: "The Colonel had no desire to keep the thing up: it was getting monotonous; but all at once there was a lull in the conflict, and the well-trained *circus horse*—for such he was—was as easily guided as the Colonel wished; but he never rode him under fire again."

27/321

The Loop Hole

On May 10, 1864, three Federal corps attacked Confederates holding entrenchments northwest of Spotsylvania Court House, Virginia. The artillery and musketry fire on this day was pretty bad, and the soldiers on both sides took it as well as they could.

Just behind the fortified line held by the Richmond Howitzers of Cabell's Battalion, Longstreet's Corps, were posted members of General Hood's Texas/Arkansas Brigade. During the battle, one company of Texans, consisting of the captain and three privates, all that was left of the original 100 men, had settled into a little shelter tent to play cards. The tent was the basic "A" style, or "pup" tent—two pieces of canvas buttoned together at the ridge pole, with another piece of canvas "lapped" across the back end, leaving a small triangle hole at the top rear about 18 inches long for ventilation. Despite the danger and noise of combat, these fellows were having a nice time engaged in a card game known as "Seven up."

Suddenly an artillery shell came screeching over, struck the ground, tumbled over once or twice, then stopped rolling right at the mouth of the tent, its fuse burning, and ready to detonate. Instantly the game stopped, and the players were up and fleeing for their lives! In a split second one of the Texans went flying head first through the small triangle hole in the rear of the tent. He was followed in quick succession by the other three, the captain coming out last. It all happened in one quick motion. And in a twinkling the four men were up and hiding behind a tree. Seconds then passed, but there was no explosion. The fuse had fizzled out, and the danger was over.

The absurdity of the scene finally hit home. One onlooker reported that everyone who had been watching was at first horrified at the certain fate of the four Texans. Then moments later their shouts of laughter filled the air, especially when it was noted that all of the men *still held on to their respective "hands"!*

Soon the shell was kicked aside, and all went back to the tent where the game was resumed. Later, the captain mused that these three men were all that was left of his entire company, and when the shell landed he thought these remainders were "gone up" for good.

36/153

Coming Through

As part of General Richard Taylor's army, Colonel Henry Gray of the 28th Louisiana commanded a brigade during the 1864 Red River Campaign. Gray, a 48-year-old lawyer, was an unpretentious gentleman, and was much loved and respected by his infantrymen. But if the truth were known, Colonel Gray had one big weakness. He simply had no respect for the Southern cavalry operating in the Trans-Mississippi, the department Gray was assigned to. To the old infantry colonel, they were less than useless, and when not trying to hide from a fight, these mounted rascals were usually out combing the countryside for something to steal or someone to bother.

After the Confederate victory at Mansfield, Louisiana on April 8, 1864, General Taylor's force was marching south, following in the wake of General N. P. Bank's retreating Federal army. By the second week in May, Taylor's men were near Cane River where they encountered stragglers from General John Wharton's ragtag Rebel cavalry division, the very troops Colonel Gray hated.

Wharton had placed a line of soldiers in rear of his division to help prevent this straggling, and had also ordered Colonel Gray to allow no horseman to pass by these guards. But somehow one of the despised cavalrymen slipped through this line, and shortly found himself face-to-face with Colonel Gray who was riding in front of his brigade. As the trooper attempted to go on by, the colonel halted him, and inquired as to "what part of the army he belonged to."

"I don't belong to the army, I belong to the cavalry."

"That's a fact," said Gray, "you can pass on."

52/166

High and Dry

The fighting around Spotsylvania, Virginia, during the middle days of May 1864, was as intense as any during the war. The front lines of the two armies were well fortified with miles of trench lines, rifle pits, artillery lunettes, traverses, and every other type of earthwork imaginable. So were the rear areas, which were honey-combed with "bomb proofs" and various shelters that afforded protection from projectiles.

Doctor William H. Cox, the surgeon of Major Poague's Artillery Battalion, was no exception to these self-preservation efforts. Desiring complete safety, he had

built a "capacious bomb proof," about 100 yards in rear of the battalion's artillery line, where Cox, according to Poague, could attend to the wounded, "without being molested" by Yankee metal.

One day nature's rain came down in torrents; it was unrelenting, and filled every depression in the ground with streams of water. During the downpour, someone remarked that the doctor had not been seen in a while, out of his "cave." With the rain continuing, a few soldiers bet that it would not be long before Cox would be forced to exit his protective lair or else be drowned. As more time passed, and no doctor, a man was sent to investigate. He found the bomb proof flooded, and the surgeon hanging to the timbers overhead, trying to keep his body out of the rising water. When asked why he had not left such an uncomfortable place, Dr. Cox replied:

"It was getting somewhat damp, but better to endure it than expose oneself needlessly."

19/93

The Good Side

The First Company, Richmond Howitzers, was said to be one of the best artillery batteries in Confederate service. However, even with its share of good and brave men, under certain circumstances the survival urge overcame all pretense of honor, glory and patriotism.

It is universally known that the musketry firing at the Battle of Spotsylvania was as deadly as any encountered during any Civil War engagement. It did not take a soldier there long to perceive the dangerous situation he occupied in those furious May days of 1864.

Sometime during this bloodly fight, one of the cannons of the "Howitzers" was run out into a very exposed position in advance of the main line. Subsequently, the gun had to be abandoned due to a destructive fire aimed at it from the Federal trenches. Later in the day, when the battery was ordered to move away, the captain directed a sergeant to take a detachment and bring in the lone piece. The sergeant and his gunner, with a few additional privates, went out to drag the cannon in by hand. Two men immediately lifted the trail of the gun carriage, and the sergeant called out, "All together!" The gun did move, but it moved *in a circle.*

Yankee bullets now began to sing through the air, over and around the men. The situation was tense, and the ground around that single cannon grew decidedly uncomfortable and very unsafe. The sergeant then saw the problem; his men were all on the *same side of the gun,* the side away from the enemy!

After some persuasion, the corporal and the sergeant induced a couple of men to move to the *other* side, and the cannon began to roll correctly. When a ball smacked the sergeant in the chest, the cannoneers bent even harder to the wheels, and the precious weapon was finally pushed and pulled to shelter.

21/109

A Bird on the Wing

This next tale is a piece of classic humor from the Civil War, and should be familiar to anyone who has read even a sprinkling of soldiers' accounts from that conflict. It has been so often repeated by various writers and editors that there is an obligation to include it here.

On May 9, 1864 a small force of about 3,500 Confederates attempted to slow the advance of a powerful Union corps led by General James B. McPherson. The place was near Resaca, Georgia on the Snake Creek Gap Road. General James Cantey, commanding the Southern force, placed the 37th Mississippi Infantry in one position near a bridge over the creek, and another regiment, the 17th Alabama, on a ridge closer in, and in front of a small breastwork occupied by the 66th Georgia under Colonel James C. Nisbet.

Soon three divisions of Federals advanced and surrounded the 37th Mississippi, causing a general retreat and the loss of many men captured. The disaster to the Mississippians demoralized the 17th Alabama, a "raw" regiment, and their resistance collapsed, as the victorious Yanks charged across the little creek. Colonel Nisbet's men at the defensive works, along with remnants of the 37th and 17th, poured a heavy fire into the enemy as they approached, but many of the 37th and 17th broke away and continued their flight rearward.

Nisbet and his Georgians tried to stop the flow by ordering and even forcing the frightened soldiers into their own firing line. In an encounter with one of his fleeing comrades-in-arms, Colonel Nisbet called out in a loud voice: "Halt! What are you running for?"

"Bekase I kain't fly!" answered the scared Reb.

Concluded the colonel. "Those that stopped held the works.... The rest may be running yet,..."

14/180 & 2/9/505

Seek and Ye Shall Find

Most brave and sensible Confederate soldiers took no more chances with their safety in battle than was prudent to perform their duties honorably and judiciously. But in the ranks of some units, there was a segment of the military population who believed in *predestination.* In short, they *said* it was no use to take precautions during combat, or to worry about danger, because what was already "ordained by God," was absolute and could not be changed or affected by the actions of humans. However, the majority of veterans in the Southern army scoffed at this idea and acted accordingly.

Colonel William Oates was one soldier who took this sensible position. He called such thinking superstitious, and commented: "I don't think that the blood of man is held in such high esteem by the Great Creator of all things as to cause him to interfere with the uniform and perfect operation of His laws for any such purpose."

These good thoughts aside, Colonel Oates did have a funny story about one such "believer" in his 15th Alabama, Private Bryant Wilson. It took place during the combat near Spotsylvania on the night of May 9, 1864:

> *Bryant was a good soldier and an excellent citizen. He was a hard-shell Baptist and believed in fate, predestination, or foreordination, and hence that he could not die until the specially appointed time for that event, and that when that time came nothing could save him. When the firing began that night he was standing at his post, but was asleep. He knew not which way to go nor what to do. He said he still had his faith, but that the balls were flying so thickly around him that he concluded to aid the Lord in his preservation by getting behind a tree. But when he got there he could not tell which was the Lord's side, as the balls seemed to be coming from every direction, hence concluded that the tree was not the particular instrumentality for his preservation on that occasion, but that flat on the ground was the chosen spot, so he took that and held it until the firing ceased.*
>
> *His faith was consoling on ordinary occasions, but on that occasion was not on each side of the tree at one and the same time; it was foreordained that he should lie on the ground and escape.*

48/132 & 358

Passing in Review

On May 12, 1864, the Battle of Spotsylvania Courthouse raged in all its demonic fury. It was unquestionably one of the most ferocious military engagements of the war. During one phase of the action, at about one p.m., the brigade that the 16th Virginia was attached to, General Mahone's, was moved to the right of the fighting line to support Lane's North Carolina brigade. This put the unit more directly in front of the old county courthouse itself.

Later in the evening, Mahone's brigade was ordered to attack the Union entrenchments. As it moved out under a severe artillery fire from the Yankees, several men in the 16th Virginia were killed and wounded. One of the injured was a popular young officer, Lieutenant Thomas W. Smith, of Co. A, who received an enemy bullet through his right thigh. Two men assisted Smith to the rear, but seeing he was too weak to walk from loss of blood, Ben Hannaford, one of the privates, helped him to the nearby courthouse building which was being utilized as an aid station. There, a surgeon told Lieutenant Smith that he would have to go to Anderson's Division hospital two miles away, as enemy shellfire was making the courthouse hospital untenable.

As Smith was still too weak to hobble much further, Hannaford found a wheelbarrow, and with assistance, made the lieutenant as comfortable as possible within. Then Hannaford said: "Now, my Lieutenant, I will roll you over to the division hospital."

As they passed by the front of the courthouse, General William N. Pendleton, Lee's chief of artillery, happened to be sitting there on a fence rail busily engaged in sending batteries to the front. The general, catching a glimpse of Smith in the wheelbarrow, hailed him and asked: "Lieutenant, what are you doing? Where are you going?" Smith, looking up at the general, raised himself up as well as he could in the one-wheel conveyance, saluted, and answered: "General, I am passing in review." The old general smiled and replied: "Go on, you will not die."

And he didn't. Smith recovered, returned to his unit and was wounded again, but survived the war.

11/132

Artistic Licentious

The uniform blouse worn by the artillerymen of the First Company, Richmond Howitzers was a short jacket, or "roundabout," which came to the waist only. Therefore any damage to the seat of the pants was immediately conspicuous. And, as can be expected, after many months of hard service, these trousers began to show considerable wear from sitting on the ground and other rough surfaces, such as tree stumps, logs, and rocks, causing holes of all sizes to show through to the bare skin or the underclothes of the men. And normally, when repairs were made by the men, they employed whatever material was at hand, ending up with a plain unpretentious patch.

However, Ben Lankert, one of the "Howitzers," was a fun-loving fellow, and was not satisfied with the mundane; he always sought something more inventive. So one morning, Ben appeared as usual at roll call, but this day he sported on his rear end, "a large patch in the shape of a heart transfixed with an arrow, done out of red flannel."

This was too much for the rest of the company. Their admiration and envy was complete:

> *Each one set his ingenuity to work to devise something unique. Soon the results began to appear. Upon the seats of one, and another, were displayed figures of birds, beasts and men—a spread eagle, a cow, a horse, a cannon. One artist depicted a "Cupid" with his bow, with an arrow from Cupid's bow— all wrought out of red flannel and sewed on as patches to cover the holes in the pants, and, at the same time, present a pleasing appearance. By and by these devices increased in number, and when the company was fallen in for roll call, the line, seen from the rear, presented a very gay and festive effect.*

One morning the Howitzers had a guest. It was General Joseph Finegan, new to the Army of Northern Virginia, and in command of a Florida brigade. As the roll was called, the general and Captain Edward McCarthy stood watching nearby. When muster was complete, the orderly sergeant gave the order, "'Bout face!'"

At this command, the backside of the line of artillerymen was immediately flipped toward General Finegan:

> *When that art gallery—in red flannel—was suddenly displayed to his delighted eyes, the General nearly laughed himself into a fit. "Oh, boys" he cried out, "don't ever turn your backs upon the enemy. Sure they'll git ye—red makes a divil of a good target. But I wouldn't have missed this for the world."*
>
> *The effect, as seen from the rear, was impressive. It could be seen a mile off—bright red patches on dull gray cloth.*

36/37

Do What?

Major William M. Owen, commanding the Washington Artillery of New Orleans, was ordered in late May 1864, to report to General Bushrod Johnson at the "Howlett House" battery on James River. There his battalion would complete a tour of duty on the battle lines opposite the enemy's forces.

The first night at his new post, Major Owen found a berth on the floor of a house General Johnson and his staff were using as headquarters. Later that evening, everyone was rudely awakened by the sound of a Yankee gunboat out on the river firing its huge 15-inch guns. The major ought to describe what happened next:

The shells flew high over the house, went beyond, and exploded. At the first report the General sat bolt upright and said, "Boys! boys! hear that? Those infernal things will hit us sure." We assured him that they did not have our range, and there was no danger; but he said, "But, boys, the blamed thing might wabble!"

We had a laugh at the General's expense, who was as brave a man as Julius Caesar. The idea of a monster gun on a monitor wabbling!

27/323

Who's Counting?

During the cavalry engagement at Trevilian's Station, Virginia on June 11, 1864, General Wade Hampton commanded a brigade in J.E.B. Stuart's Cavalry Division. At one point in the fighting, Hampton ordered a counter-attack which routed a Yankee thrust that had nearly succeeded in capturing Captain James F. Hart's Battery, a Confederate artillery unit participating in the battle. In this spirited charge, Hampton led the 6th South Carolina Cavalry, telling them beforehand: "Mount your horses, men, and follow me." Moments later the Federals were routed; they turned and rode furiously to the rear. In hot pursuit was General Hampton, who shot two Northern soldiers out of their saddles.

Many years afterwards, in May 1901, ex-Confederate Ulysses R. Brooks of the 6th was visiting with the general, and asked how many of the enemy he had killed during the war. Hampton answered, "eleven,—two with the sword and nine with a pistol."

Brooks then retorted: "How about the two at Trevilian's Station?" Hampton replied: "O, I didn't count them; they were running."

2/22/409

A Wig Wag

Union General David Hunter began a retreat westward after the Battle of Lynchburg, Virginia, which was fought on June 7-8, 1864. There Hunter had been repulsed by Confederates under Generals John Breckenridge and Jubal Early. The Rebels followed the Yankees closely, engaging the enemy's rearguard whenever possible. One of the units in General Early's advance, and the regiment this story is centered around, was the 6th Virginia Cavalry.

In one of these delaying actions which occurred near Beauford's Gap, a small portion of the 6th was commanded by John N. Opie. In this engagement, Opie was supposed to cooperate with a force called Davis' Battalion Virginia Cavalry, led by Major Thomas S. Davis. In the ensuing skirmish, however, everything possible that could go wrong, did.

According to Opie, Major Davis appeared to have given him the wrong information and location of the Federals. And since the country was dense, and mountainous, it was very hard to see and maneuver. But finally, after many harrowing and tiring hours, Opie's men, with aid from another company, were able to drive the Yanks back onto a main road, where Davis was supposed to attack them.

Unfortunately, Davis' Battalion failed to appear, so Opie brought his men out of the woods and down to the foot of the mountain. There his troopers sat and waited for the consolidation of all the commands.

Sometime later, as Opie's little force rested, Major Davis rode up, and in a loud and angry voice demanded: "Why in the hell didn't you hold your position on the mountain?"

In reply to the question, Opie countered, "Why in the hell didn't you charge on the main road with your regiment...?"

Davis shot back, in a tone suggesting that Opie had left too soon: "*I* would have staid there as long as there was a hair on my head."

Just then Private Thomas Marshall, who was a member of Opie's company, stepped forward. His head was as bare as a billiard ball, because in coming down the thick, tangled hillside, he had lost his wig. Upon hearing Davis' insulting observation, Marshall, who was a great wag, took off his hat and bowed to Davis with much mock politeness, and said: "[Major], *we* did."

25/243

Deep Enough

In the fall of 1864, Colonel Henry L. Giltner's Kentucky Cavalry Brigade was made aware that a distinguished guest was going to be visiting in the vicinity of their campground and would be there to pay his respects on a certain day. This well-known personage was former Confederate general, Humphrey Marshall, who once commanded the 1st Kentucky Cavalry, but had resigned his position earlier in the war. Marshall, a West Point graduate and lawyer, had since become a member of the Second Confederate Congress in Richmond.

The guest eventually arrived, but was a day late, and since the ex-general, now congressman, was fond of the "stump," he was invited to make a speech to the men of the brigade. Marshall began his oration by complimenting his fellow Kentuckians for their achievements and conduct, and stated that he always kept an ear open as to their movements and welfare. He waxed eloquently, apologizing to them for not coming sooner, but said he had been with them in spirit. In fact, Marshall confessed, "he had met a few convivial spirits and got too much in the spirit, or too much of the spirit in himself....etc." So, as he said, in moving about the various camps he had gotten a bit mixed up, and the hospitality had flowed so freely that he could scarcely get things straightened out. At any rate he was here now, and wanted to make it up to the boys.

General Marshall's speech then grew even more poetic and grand. He inspired the men of Kentucky to stand firm, and fight on until the war was fought to a glorious and triumphant conclusion, "even though it became necessary to wade waist-deep in blood."

At this juncture, an interruption of the tipsy orator was made. The interrupter was Captain Barney Giltner, a cousin and aid-de-camp to the brigade commander. He was tall, educated, with a well-formed physique, and was always immaculately clean and well-dressed. He had, too, a great wit, and was considered the brigade philosopher, whose quaint sayings, apropos quotations, witticisms, clever songs, convivial facial expressions, and splenetic observations, were so irresistible that they kept the men laughing even when discomforts and tribulations bore them down.

It was then that Barney Giltner shouted out his comment, which "brought down the house:"

"General, that's too deep for me. I only contracted to go in *knee deep*."

7/94 & 192

A Bad Plan

A few hours before the Federals occupied Fort Smith on September 1, 1864, a squad of Confederates were sent to act as a rear guard at the crossing of the Arkansas River. Being somewhat understrength, the little Rebel force decided to take along a small cannon they had recently found. The gun had no carriage, so the men strapped the artillery tube to the back of a large mule.

When the Southerners reached the river, Yankee soldiers could be seen on the west side of the stream preparing to cross over. To slow the enemy up, the cannon was loaded and aimed, and when all was ready, the newly appointed gunner sounded out: "Match her off."

Up to this time the old mule had stood pretty steady, with the barrel on his back pointed toward the Yanks. But when the match was touched to the fuse, and began to sizzle and fizzle, and hot sparks fell upon his neck and withers, the animal became very excited. He started turning round and round in terror, causing

the gun to swivel about and point in all directions except the one intended. The Confederates all hit the ground and scurried for cover from the careening mule, shouting, "Down, boys!"

Hearing the commotion, their captain rushed to the scene. Seeing the Union troops in the distance, and his scattered command, he called out: "Up and into line, boys!" But no one stirred. The order came again and again with deeper emphasis, until Private Sam Moore, replied: "Up and thunder and lightening! We will stay down till that mule shoots."

In another instant the cannon fired, the mule tumbled down upon his knees, and the shell struck and exploded on a nearby hillside, far from its mark. The captain then cried out, "Every man take care of himself; they are all around us."

The laugh was on the captain, and all retreated in good order, including the mule and gun.

2/9/309

Thanks, But No Thanks

Private Philip D. Stephenson, a member of the 5th Company, Washington Artillery, became sick with dysentery in late September 1864, after hard service in the Atlanta Campaign. He was sent to a hospital at Forsyth, Georgia and due to the influence of several friends was allowed to recuperate in the officer's ward of that facility. Another man staying in the large tent Stephenson occupied was a comrade from Virginia, Captain Thomas W. Bartlett of Company K, 13th Arkansas Infantry.

One thing Stephenson noted in his time as a patient, was that the local women who nursed the soldiers usually gave most of their attention and sympathy to the *wounded* men, rather than those who were only ill. But according to Stephenson, overall the *care* for both sick and wounded was excellent. Captain Bartlett came under special scrutiny by the nurses, but for obvious reasons, he did not wish for their close examinations:

> *Captain Bartlett's experience with [these women] was...amusing. He was wounded and badly, and they actually swarmed around him! In addition to*

being wounded, the gallant captain was handsome and had most captivating manners, that mixture of deference and audacity which ladies love. His wound was in the fleshy part of his anatomy generally regarded as unmentionable to female ears, and their questions kept him in a fever of embarrassment. "Where were you wounded?" "At Atlanta, ma'am," but that didn't satisfy. Presently the conversation would be brought around again, "Where did you say you were wounded?" "At Atlanta, madam!" would come out again, half mischievously, half desperately. Well he knew the persistency of female curiosity and also female sympathy, *and that the next question ever pending was,* "Don't you want me to dress your wound?"

This was a daily fire which he had to face until the sight of the ladies tempted him almost to duck his head under the cover and play dead.

53/249

"Pan" Demonium

A week after the Battle of Fort Harrison, Virginia on September 29, 1864, a place where General Lee's forces had attempted to retake a line of fortifications captured by the Federals, the 4th Alabama Infantry, along with other units in the same area were ordered by Lee to attack a Union cavalry division.

The Yankees were commanded by General August V. Kautz and were in an exposed and partially entrenched position on the Darbytown Road near Richmond, north of the James River. When the assault was made, the Confederates were initially successful in breaking directly into the enemy cavalry's bivouac.

"The men went yelling, running and firing right through horses, wagons, cannon and camp, [Union] troopers fleeing in every direction. It was a regular picnic for the boys" reported Adjutant Robert Cole of the 4th Alabama. "Major William M. Robbins cried out, 'Look boys, I've at last found a prize worth fighting for.' Holding aloft a frying pan with a good long handle and waving it in lieu of his sword, he cheered and urged the men forward, and appeared to value his capture immensely, until a bullet from one of Kautz's repeating Spencer rifles, with a 'ping,' went through the bottom of it,..."

Major Robbins seeing the hole, threw the pan down and looking at it with sadness, exclaimed: "Yes, it was ever thus; from childhood's hour I've seen my fondest hopes decay."

47/186

Heaven Sent

To many soldiers who served in the Confederate army during the war years of 1861-1865, it was comforting to believe that there was a power watching over and guiding them through the horrors of battle and the various accidents and misfortunes of daily life. For many others who were skeptics, it seemed mighty peculiar that *some* men were killed or wounded, or succumbed to death by disease and other causes, while other individuals remained healthy and untouched by the deadly missiles of destruction. Furthermore, and most importantly, the religious nature of the person involved did not seem to alter the fact of whom would be next to fall.

Randolph McKim may have thought he could answer that age-old mystery, for he was a soldier who became a preacher during the war, and later served as a chaplain in the 2nd Virginia Cavalry. A humorous incident related by McKim, which happened at the Battle of Cedar Creek in October 1864, brought the mystery again into question, but as usual there came no answer:

> *At one stage of the fight, a squadron of the regiment was drawn up behind a little slope, mounted and ready to charge when needed. The enemy was feeling for us with artillery, and the shells were dropping uncomfortably near. I rode to the front of the squadron, drew out my little Psalm book,...and offered prayer for the divine blessing and protection, the men reverently removing their hats. When I had finished, the commanding officer moved the squadron about twenty or thirty yards to a spot which he thought less exposed. No sooner was the movement executed than a shell came hurtling through the air, struck the ground and exploded on the very spot we had just left. The men exchanged glances at this, and I heard one of the roughest of the troopers say to another, "Bill, I say, that does look like an answer to pra'ar, doesn't it?"*

15/235

(Unfortunately, another 6,000 Union and Confederate soldiers, withheld from the heavenly influence and intercession of Reverend McKim, were killed or maimed at Cedar Creek....)

Roddey's Rap

There were a few units in both armies during the war that built reputations for avoiding enemy fire if at all possible. Such a regiment must have been the Union's 5th Tennessee Cavalry, known as "Stokes' Cavalry" after its commander William B. Stokes. General Nathan B. Forrest had so little respect for this organization, that once when he had surrounded a town and was about to open fire on the Union troops therein, he sent a message to the mayor to remove Stokes' Cavalry, along with the women and children, as he did not want to shoot non-combatants.

The Southern army had a similar regiment in the 4th Alabama Cavalry, or "Roddey's Cavalry," led by Colonel Philip D. Roddey. On one occasion a railroad train was passing through Alabama carrying a large number of Rebel soldiers, one among them who had had a personal experience with, or had heard of, the poor record made by Roddey's men. This infantryman, who was sitting at the front end of a car, rose from his seat, gun in hand, and asked in a loud voice if there were any members of Roddey's Regiment on board. There was no reply, so he repeated the question with more insistence. This time an affirmative, but softly worded response came from a wary little fellow at the far end of the railroad car.

"That's all right, then," said the inquiring foot soldier with an air of great relief, as he cocked his musket and shoved the muzzle out of the window. "I just wanted to tell you not to be scared honey, for I ain't a bit mad; I'm only gwine ter pop a cap."

2/5/292 & 425

Sweet Revenge

On October 21, 1864, the Army of Tennessee halted for a time on its northward campaign march, and was bivouacked in the vicinity of Gadsden, Alabama. While in camp that evening, the officers and men were serenaded by army bands, and speeches were given by various commanders, including Generals Beauregard, Cleburne, Clayton, and Bate. The last named individual particularly stood out that night by a little poem he constructed in response to an order issued by the governor of Georgia. General William B. Bate was a Mexican War veteran who was then serving as a division commander in the Southern army. He had studied law before the war, and had worked as a newspaper editor and Tennessee legislator. Bate, like others on the front line of battle, was angered by the actions of Governor Joseph Brown, who had, in each county of his state, just exempted from service a large number of military age citizens for the purpose of raising provisions for the army, sorghum being named as one of the products to be so used. (*Sorghum* is a type of "cereal grass" with a sweet, juicy stalk, similar to sugar cane, grown for grain, fodder, syrup, etc., and was a staple commodity in the South.) The fighting men of the Confederacy were appalled that civilians would be excused from duty to their country, then in its greatest time of need, to raise crops like sorghum.

So, General Bate, known for his eloquence and wit, and with this little gem, became the toast of the evening orators:

> *What tho destruction sweep these lovely plains,*
> *Who cares for liberty while sorghum yet remains?*
> *With that sweet name we wave our knives on high,*
> *And swear to cut it while we live, and suck it till we die.*

39/167 & 53/247

Cage's Catharsis

Early in the war it was not uncommon to encounter dozens of black slaves in many of the Southern regiments who acted as personal servants, cooks, etc., and even sometimes as "fighters." As the conflict progressed, the total slave population in the army declined somewhat as many were sent home, but slaves were present in some units even up to the final surrenders. It was also normal for slave owners to "rotate" their servants periodically, which allowed visits to families back home on farms and plantations throughout the South.

In one regiment of General Joseph B. Kershaw's South Carolina Brigade, an officer's young cook was sent home "on rotation." Replacing him was an older man named "Uncle Cage." Days before Cage left for the army, he had listened to the just returned younger man tell stories of the bloody battlefields, the cannon's roar and the screaming of the shells, as they sought out even the "safe" refuge of the cooks, the rear areas back at the "wagon yards." One of these tales even involved the demise of a cook who lost his head when it was shot off by a cannonball. Although Uncle Cage's own head was quickly filled with these blood and thunder war stories, he would only chuckle and shake his head, conceding: "Dey may kill me, but dey can't skeer dis nigger."

Finally the day arrived when Cage reached camp and began his new duties. It soon came to pass that one morning, while he was preparing the breakfast meal for the officers' mess, a few "bomb shells" flew over and exploded, causing quite a commotion. Some of the more prudent cooks and other non-combatants began to seek safety by heading for the wagon yard. But Uncle Cage remained at his post, and was just saying, "Dese yer young niggers ain't no account. dey's skeered of dere own shad...." Just then, Boom! boom! and a shell detonated right over his head, throwing its deadly iron fragments all around.

Cage immediately ducked, turned, and made a beeline for the rear, calling out as he ran: "Oh, dem cussed Yankees! You want er kill er nudder nigger, don't you?" Observing soldiers and servants laughing as he flew by, "Uncle," in an attempt to rescue his pride, yelled back defiantly: "You can laff, if you want to, but old mars ain't got no niggers to fling away."

54/429

Run With This

General Jubal A. Early was a man who had a most curious sense of humor, and had the remarkable ability to say clever things in an understated way. For instance, one day during the Spotsylvania Campaign he rode up to the *regimental* headquarters of the 1st Maryland Cavalry, and found the colonel, the adjutant, and the other officers all enjoying personal sleeping tents and other extra camp comforts, even a mess tent. Knowing that General Lee, in the spring of 1864, had severely restricted the amount of baggage his army could carry, and the Marylanders were clearly exceeding the letter of the regulation, Early exclaimed in a leisurely, quaint way: "What army *corps* headquarters is this?"

Several months later, during the Shenandoah Valley Campaign in early November 1864, "Old Jube" had an opportunity to use this style of humor on General Thomas Rosser, who commanded Early's cavalry during a portion of the campaign.

By this date in 1864, the cavalry of the Confederate army rarely had the power to gain any advantage over the enemy, but Rosser's troopers were especially impotent against the strong and well-equipped Yankee horsemen of General Philip Sheridan's forces in the valley.

In the later part of the campaign, General Rosser, who led what was called the "Laurel Brigade," had been beaten by General George A. Custer's Federal cavalry at Woodstock and Cedar Creek, and other smaller engagements, causing them to be constantly in retreat before the much superior U.S. mounted units.

About this time, and after these disastrous encounters, General Early's attention was attracted by the "green sprigs" worn in the hats of Rosser's men, and asked the significance. Someone, in explanation, said, "Why, General, don't you know they call their command the 'Laurel brigade' and these are sprigs of laurel."

Old Jubal in his calm way didn't miss the que, and quickly retorted: "I never knew the laurel was a *running* plant, I think a pumpkin vine would be more appropriate."

44/152

The Power to Heal

John S. Robson of the 52nd Virginia Infantry, became a one-legged Rebel in October 1864, at the Battle of Cedar Creek. During the fight he was acting as a mounted courier for General John Pegram, a division commander under General Jubal Early.

After his wounding and subsequent amputation, Robson was sent to a large military hospital to recuperate. While in this facility, he noted that the teasing and joking between the patients and doctors seem to do more for the health of the soldiers than the medicine they were given. To illustrate this belief, and to highlight the fun-loving attitude of the staff, he told this little anecdote:

> One case...reported was that of a man brought in, dangerously wounded in three places. After the examination by the surgeon, an assistant asked: "Doctor, is the man badly hurt?" "Yes," said the surgeon, "two of the wounds are mortal, but the third can be cured, provided the man is kept perfectly quiet for six weeks."

22/149

Horse Cents

For a man who was under enemy fire 179 times during his 46 months of service to the Confederacy, and who rose from private soldier to lieutenant general, it would at first appear that he could not have had much of a sense of humor. But on the contrary, Nathan Bedford Forrest was well-known for his humorous side, and his fondness for a joke, or a good laugh, when the occasion permitted it.

Captain John P. Young of the 7th Tennessee Cavalry was an aid to Forrest, and once related the facetious side of the general. During a skirmish on November 29, 1864, at Mount Carmel, Tennessee, just prior to the Battle of Franklin. General Forrest had just dismounted after coming under a hot fire from Yankee musketry. According to Young:

> *[He] sat down on a rock, an example which was quickly followed by the writer, who was attending him, and who took care to get down on the opposite side of his horse from the enemy. The General, who had begun feeding his warhorse, "King Philip," with some blades of fodder he found there, turned, and, observing my point of vantage, playfully said, "You had better get on the other side of that horse, bud, and stop the bullets. Horses are lots scarcer than men out here."—a suggestion, by the way, that was not followed.*

2/5/278

1865-1897

One Last Shot

It was well known by the Southern populace that the president of the Confederacy, Jefferson Davis, suffered from severe eye problems, especially with herpes in his left eye, which caused him to be practically blind on some days.

A soldier in the 5th Company Washington Artillery described Davis' face as thoughtful, with sunken cheeks and delicate features. "One eye was gone, which however did not show except that 'the light was out' and the lid drooped over it a little."

The commander of the Army of Tennessee, whom Davis had appointed, had his own problems. General John B. Hood lived with the disability of an arm injured at Gettysburg, and a leg lost at the Battle of Chickamauga. How these two "medical situations" could have anything in common, is the purpose of this story, and comes down from a worn out Rebel soldier during the harsh winter of 1864-1865.

The Army of Tennessee under General Hood had suffered a string of defeats near Atlanta, and more recently at Franklin and Nashville. By early January, the soldiers of that once fine army were in the grip of their lowest morale ever. All around them, Union armies were crushing any force the Confederacy could muster; food and clothing was scarce, the weather was brutally cold and wet, and these troops were in full retreat. The situation looked very bleak indeed.

As the army plodded southward through the mud and slush after the Battle of Nashville, many of the men were barefoot and poorly clothed, and a freezing rain did not help their spirits. Among this throng of disgruntled, broken-down infantrymen was a gaunt, hungry Tennessean, who probably summed up the whole miserable situation best. He had just fallen into a mud-hole and was dragging himself out, and what he said to his comrades likely represented their feelings exactly:

Draft 'Em!

The summer and fall of 1864 had been hard on General Jubal A. Early's small but brave army. For five months he had fought and maneuvered against General Philip S. Sheridan and other superior forces in or out of the Shenandoah Valley. In the end, Early's troops had been beaten, and the valley fell to the invaders. But even as late as November 10, Early had again tried to intimidate Sheridan. But with no reinforcements, and his tiny, understrength army weakened by sending regiments to fortify Richmond and Petersburg, this attempt was a failure against the hoards of well-armed and equipped Yankees. And remarkably, since June, Early's men had marched almost 1,700 miles and fought nearly 75 engagements of one kind or another. So, with 1864 past and the Shenandoah Valley Campaign history, his Confederates rested and refitted near New Market.

On Sunday, January 15, 1865. General Early, whose headquarters were then in Staunton, decided to attend church. During the sermon, the preacher, in speaking of the dead of the centuries past, asked his audience, with great dramatic effort, what would they do if the dead came marching back to earth by thousands and tens of thousands?

And out in the congregation, at this very inspiring moment, came the semi-audible answer of "Old Jube," who, doubtless, was thinking of his feeble little army and the hopelessness of getting reinforcements: "I'd conscript every damned one of them."   33/324

Granny Was a Load

The weeks and months between the defeat of the Confederate Army of Tennessee at the Battles of Franklin and Nashville in the winter of 1864, through to the spring of 1865, was the most difficult period faced by that army during the entire war. The specter of their recent losses, combined with the harsh winter, and the lack of proper rations and clothing, led to the demoralization of the soldiers, and the belief that they were witnessing the "Death Knell of the Confederacy."

But through it all, many Rebels kept their sense of humor. Lieutenant Robert Collins of the 15th Texas, proved this through a little narrative he told of an ancient pig his men caught near Augusta, Georgia in February, 1865:

Our fare [had been] lean indeed. The day we arrived on the banks of the Tiger river [I] carried Jim Hardin's gun, ammunition and luggage while he would go miles out on either side of the road in quest of something to eat. Late in the evening he came in, not having found a thing. The writer was now commanding Company "B" and had just five men in his company, and we all started out on a foraging excursion, and the only thing we found in all that country was an old sow, solitary and alone. She [had] a powerful big frame but [was] very poor. We slaughtered her, and after taking her hide off, the

*middlings were about as thick and tough as your shoe soles, and had about
the same amount of grease in them. When we put the meat on to fry we would
have to put on the skillet lid to keep it from jumping out. We made supper and
breakfast on it, put the remainder in a sack, and the boys took turns in carrying it until we ate it up. When a fellow would get tired you would hear him
say, "Here Jim, I am tired; it is your time to carry Grandmother awhile...."*

49/283

At Your Service, Ma'am

One of the most interesting weddings of the war took place in Richmond on
January 19, 1865, in St. Paul's Church. There, Hetty Cary of Baltimore married
General John Pegram, a division commander in Lee's army. A friend of the groom
described Pegram as one of the "most lovable and handsomest men" he knew.
Miss Cary was complimented by the same officer, as "the most beautiful woman
I ever saw in any land.... With her classic face, her pure complexion, her auburn
hair, [and] her perfect figure...."

A few days after the ceremony, on February 2, General John B. Gordon held
a military review for Pegram's Division. In reality, it was also an occasion "to
parade the bride," as everyone in the army was anxious to see or meet Pegram's
lovely new spouse. Many notables were present, including Generals Robert E.
Lee, James Longstreet, Richard Anderson, Henry Heth, and others. When the division passed in review, General Gordon abdicated his duty, and allowed Mrs.
Pegram to receive the salute of the troops. The adjutant general of the division
described this unusual moment:

> *General Lee was on her right and the other generals with their glittering
> staff officers about her and in her train. Her rich color emblazoned her face,
> a rare light illumined her eyes and her soul was on fire with the triumph of
> the moment, the horrors of war forgotten. I rode with her off the field, and as
> we passed the troops returning to camp, she was sitting her horse like the Maid
> of France and smiling upon them with her marvelous beauty, their wild enthu-
> siasm sought in vain for fitting expression and vent. An excited "Tar Heel,"
> whom her horse struck and nearly knocked down, quickly sprang up and, as
> she reined up her horse and began to apologize, he broke in as he seized his
> old hat from his head.*
>
> *"Never mind, Miss. You might have rid all over me, indeed you might!"*

33/326

Pickles' Personal Plea

In February 1865, after nearly four years of combat, the "civil war" in America
was fast drawing to a close, and many Southern soldiers could feel the Confederacy tottering on its last legs. In these trying times, even brave men thought twice
about sacrificing their lives so near to the end. It is very likely that just such an
attitude prompted the following event.

One day early in that bleak month, General Henry Heth's Confederate Division came upon a portion of the Federal army firmly entrenched far out on the Squirrel Level Road, southeast of Petersburg, Virginia. The Yankees, with a battery of artillery, were well posted on an imposing eminence. General Heth, after halting his force, rode up to General William McComb, commanding Archer's Tennessee Brigade, and notified him that he wanted some of McComb's sharpshooters to advance and pick off the enemy's gunners so they could not operate their cannons. Meanwhile, the rest of the brigade would charge and capture the position. General Heth then pointed to the ugly-looking guns frowning over the earthworks, turned to McComb and gave some specific, and emphatic instructions: "We must take that battery."

When Heth had finished, a long lanky fellow named Jim Tunnage, also known as "Pickles," of Company C, 7th Tennessee Infantry walked over to General McComb. "Pickles," who had been an attentive listener to the conversation between the two generals, with much trepidation, asked McComb if we "sure enough had to take that battery." The general quietly answered, "Yes, Tunnage."

In reply to this ominous situation, "Pickles" retorted: "General don't you think we have got artillery enough? I will go and tell 'Old Heth' that if you say so."

2/7/37

Clueless

In late March 1865, General John B. Gordon was placed in command of General Lee's plan to attack and break the Union siege lines encircling Petersburg, Virginia. Just prior to this important event, now known as "the attack on Fort Stedman," General Gordon, General Henry Heth, and other officers gathered together at a little schoolhouse near the front to pray for success.

Stockton Heth, called "Sol" by his friends, was General Heth's brother, and the adjutant-general of the division. He was fondly known too, as a man always on the lookout for something "stronger than water" to drink. The day of the prayer meeting at the school, Sol was standing a short distance away, and Henry Peyton, one of General Lee's staff, beckoned to him to come to the building and join them in their pious exhortations. But Sol did not understand the object of Peyton's "hand wave" invitation. Therefore, misconstruing the real meaning, he held up his canteen, and shaking it, called out: "No, I thank you; I have just got hold of some."

3/346 & 13/416

It's a Woman Thing

The week of the retreat of General Lee's army from Petersburg and Richmond to its capitulation at Appomattox Court House, Virginia, in early April 1865, was hard and dispiriting on the enlisted men and officers of that once strong and victorious army. And following the surrender itself, the Confederates were paroled, and the long walk home began for many of them.

But some of General Lee's men did not give up at Appomattox. Feeling unconquered and with the will to fight on, a few soldiers attempted to slip through the U.S. lines and make their way southward to General Joseph E. Johnston's Army of Tennessee in North Carolina, in order to continue the war. However, the way to Johnston was full of obstacles and problems for these already exhausted and hungry men.

One day, a soldier in one of these squads, saw a comrade nearly overcome with all that he had been through, and all the unknowns ahead. The poor fellow sat with his elbows on his knees and his face in his hands. The friend accosted him, saying, "Hello, John, what is the matter with you?"

"O, I was just thinking," replied John.

"Well, what in the world were you thinking so deeply about that you were lost to every other environment?"

"Well, Jim, to tell you the truth, I was thinking I wished I was a woman."

"Wish you were a woman! Great Scotts, John, are you gone crazy? A brave soldier like you wishing to be a woman!"

"Now, Jim, I'll tell you the truth; if I were a woman I could cry as much as I pleased, and no one would think that I was a fool."

54/459

It's a Lie!

General Fitzhugh Lee, a nephew of Robert E. Lee, was in command of the decimated Cavalry Corps of the Army of Northern Virginia during the latter part of the Siege of Petersburg, and through the final Appomattox Campaign. While General Lee was arranging the surrender of his army to Generals Grant and Meade at Appomattox Court House, on April 8-9, 1865, Fitzhugh Lee and part of his command broke through the Federal army and attempted an escape. But the end had come, and two days later he and his men gave up the fight at Farmville, a few miles away.

Following his own capitulation, Fitz Lee began his journey home. Soon after the trip commenced, and while riding down a country lane, he met a veteran North Carolina infantryman, musket on his shoulder, moving along at a good pace. "Ho, there," cried General Lee, "where are you going?"

"I've been off on a furlough, and am now going back to join Gen. Bob Lee," replied the soldier.

"You needn't go back, but can throw your gun away and return home, for Lee's surrendered."

"Lee's surrendered?"

"That's what I said," said General Lee.

"It must have been that damned Fitz Lee, then. Rob Lee would never surrender," and the old soldier, tightened his grip on the rifle, put on a look of contempt, and walked on.

2/4/23

A Fine Set of Men

A humorous story which became a favorite with the former members of the Army of Northern Virginia following the Civil War, was recorded by General John B. Gordon in his 1903 reminiscences. It is presented here as he related it:

Since the war some...privates have told with great relish of the old farmer near Appomattox who decided to give employment, after the surrender, to any of Lee's veterans who might wish to work a few days for food and small wages. He divided the Confederate employees into squads according to the respective ranks held by them in the army. He was uneducated, but entirely loyal to the Southern Cause. A neighbor inquired of him as to the different squads: "Who are those men working over there?"

"Them is privates, sir, of Lee's army."

"Who are those in the second group?"

"Them is lieutenants and captains, and they works fairly well, but not as good workers as the privates."

"I see you have a third squad: who are they?"

"Them is colonels."

"Well, what about the colonels? How do they work?"

"Now, neighbor, you'll never hear me say one word ag'in' any man who fit in the Southern army; but I ain't a-gwine to hire no generals."

13/453

We're Innocent

On October 9, 1864, George M. Neese had the misfortune of being captured by Yankees led by General George Custer at Tom's Creek, near Fisher's Hill, Virginia, while serving as a gunner in Captain Roger P. Chew's Horse Artillery Battery, of Stuart's Cavalry Division. He remained a prisoner of war at Point Lookout, Maryland, until June 30, 1865. While in the army, Neese had kept a daily diary, and on April 15, 1865, wrote down these interesting notes, which disclose the undying wit of some soldiers even under the most dire of circumstances:

April 15—The United States flags here were all floating at half-mast today. This morning when the Yankee sergeant came in to superintend the roll-call he tried to look sad, but from his snappish demeanor I at once saw that the biggest bunch of his grief was entirely composed of anger. After roll-call one of the prisoners in our company ventured the question: "Sergeant, why are the flags floating at half-mast this morning?" With a scowl-covered countenance the sergeant snappishly replied: "Some of you Rebels killed President Lincoln last night." With quick repartee our man replied: "We did not do it, for we were in this pen all night."

18/353

Ya'll Can Go On Home Now

As stated in this book's introduction, during the war a fierce competitive spirit existed between the Confederate infantry and the cavalry. Both branches of service heaped abusive epithets upon each other whenever convenient, with the "infants" usually winning these contests.

In the end, in one place at least, the "doughboys" got in a last shot, and the cavalry, as usual, was bested in the exchange. It all happened in the Union prisoner-of-war camp at Ft. Delaware, located several miles below Philadelphia on Pea Patch Island. The constant topic of conversation for the Rebel prisoners, of course, was what would happen to them now that the conflict was over. The answer came from Peter Akers, a bright, witty, and mischievous captive, who walked into the prison barracks one morning, waving a newspaper, saying, "Boys, it is all settled. The [US] government has determined our fate."

His fellow prisoners, eager to learn the news, gathered around Akers, who mounted a wooden box and began to read:

> *War Department,*
> *Washington, D.C., May 25, 1865*
>
> GENERAL ORDER, No. 4320:
>
> *The following disposition will be made of the prisoners of war now confined in the various prisons of the United States, to-wit: Those who served in the Rebel infantry will be formed into two lines at the respective prisons and every tenth man will be shot to death; the remainder will be transported to the Dry Tortugas. All prisoners who served in the Rebel artillery will be deported without decimation. Whereas, this Department has received no information tending to prove that those prisoners of war who served in the Rebel cavalry, took an active part in the war against the government, or rendered any aid or comfort to the States in rebellion, it is therefore hereby ordered that they be furnished transportation to their respective homes."*

25/55

Practice What It Preaches

Almost any American can recite a short history of *Arlington*, the Virginia estate of Robert E. Lee. The house was built by George Washington's step-son, John Parke Custis and passed into Lee's possession through his wife's father, George Washington Custis. It was seized by the Federal government when Lee resigned from the army, and many of the family possessions were looted by Union soldiers. Eventually, restitution was made to the Lee family, and part of the grounds are now a National Cemetery.

After the war, General Lee received a letter from a woman who lived out west informing him that she had the Arlington family bible. Her letter suggested that if he wrote her and made claim to it, she might return it to his ownership.

Randolph H. McKim, a Marylander and former Confederate soldier, wrote that upon reading the letter, Lee's response was that, "he would not disturb the lady on the subject, adding, with that quiet humor which distinguished him, that if she would read the Good Book and reflect upon its precepts, perhaps she would restore it of her own accord."

15/166

The Namesake

One day while scouting enemy positions between Union and Confederate lines in Virginia, General Wade Hampton came across a lone Union soldier taking a bath in a stream, the Yankee believing that there were no Rebels anywhere in the vicinity. Hampton "had the drop" on the poor Yank, and quietly explained to the awestruck man that he was now a prisoner of war. Using every argument he could, the unfortunate soldier pleaded for mercy, and begged to be set free to return to his comrades bivouacked nearby.

General Hampton "played his fish" for a while, enjoying the discomfort of the wet, bare-skinned "Fed." Finally, after a little more fun, the general relented and told the captive he could go. Upon hearing those sweet words, the man thanked Hampton profusely, waded ashore, and set about to dress himself. "But the General said: 'Ah, no; I can't let you have them. My men are too much in need of clothes. I can't spare them.' After fruitless entreaties the Yankee soldier finally left for his camp as naked as when he was born, and the last words heard from him were: 'I'll name my first son Wade Hampton.'"

Years after the war, then U.S. Senator Hampton was entering an elevator in a Washington, D. C. hotel, when a young man caught up to him and said: "Are you General Hampton?" On replying in the affirmative, the stranger asked if he recalled the incident related above, along with the appropriate time and place. "Yes, I remember it perfectly," answered the senator. "Well," said the stranger, "he is my father. My name is Wade Hampton."

2/22/497

And So It Was

The late post-war years were not times when ex-Confederate soldiers hid from their military service records. In fact, there was an abundance of veteran related activities, such as reunions, parades, publication of books and articles, and the like. It was a time of flattery, and feeling good about the war, and for hand-shaking and back-slapping and all around general nostalgia, reminiscence and exaggeration. The old men in gray were all heading down that long road to oblivion, and they wanted to go out in style. Therefore, it is a rare moment when something comes from that era which dampens the bragging and the petty misrepresentations which were present in that genial atmosphere of hero-worship, comradeship, and well-meaning and harmless bravado. It is even rarer when this contradictory attitude comes from a Texan!

The 8th Texas Cavalry, also known as the 1st Texas Rangers or Terry's Texas Rangers, was a unit with an enviable record and reputation. From its organization in late 1861, to final surrender on April 26, 1865, the regiment would have made any Southerner proud to have been a part of its history. One of the 8th's most notable members was Gustave Cook, who rose from a private in the ranks to full colonel, and following the war, made an honorable name for himself in post-war Texas. But these facts are barely perceived from a letter Colonel Cook wrote in May, 1897, to his friend and former army companion, Captain J.K.P. Blackburn, outlining his life's story.

This unusual missive is captivating by its directness, understated strength, subtle humor, and rare lack of showmanship. Was it tongue-in-cheek? The reader may decide.

Dear Blackburn: You ask for a sketch of my life to go with my picture. My dear friend, it could not possibly be of slightest service or interest to the present or any future generation. The truth is, I never did nor said anything worthy of record in either civil or military life. I have made an indifferent citizen and set no example worthy of imitation.

I was born in Alabama, but the state was not to blame. I had every means, facility, and opportunity to get an education, but failed utterly even to try. I came to Texas when a boy, without any business or any particular capacity to do anything. I worked for wages, studied a little by myself, and acquired what little smattering of education I have. Just before the war I flattered myself that I could succeed at the bar and began the study of law. I enlisted in our regiment and served out my time. By some fortuitous circumstances I became orderly sergeant, captain, and then, by the death and resignation of those above me, became regularly major, lieutenant-colonel, and finally colonel of the regiment. I could have picked out a hundred men in the ranks of our command better qualified in every respect to command the regiment, and any one of whom would have done better for the country and the men than I. I was wounded several times by the carelessness of the Yankees, for I am sure that I never failed in using every precaution and prudence to avoid getting hurt.

I came home after the war and went back to the law. By reason of personal partiality for me Gov. Coke appointed me to the district bench, which I occupied for fourteen years without having done anything worthy of note outside of the usual routine.... I forgot to mention that I was sent from Harris and Montgomery Counties to the Thirteenth Legislature during reconstruction times, and drew my salary regularly during the session.

My picture flatters me very much now, for I am in very weak health, quite thin, and am getting very white....

God bless my old comrades! Give them my love. I have four children and fifteen grandchildren. In this I have been moderately successful, and possibly have not lived entirely in vain.

[Gustave Cook]

2/5/254

THE END

The Day Before Appomattox

Jackson and Hill and Stuart
Had been taken home to God,
And half our best and bravest
Were sleeping under the sod.

Onward came the army of Grant—
German and Swede and Finn,
Yankee and Dane and Dutchman—
Like a torrent pouring in.

But we held our lines of battle,
Though they charged us ten to one;
And our crimson cross was flying
At the setting of the sun.

But still they swarmed around us,
Negro and Pole and Hun,
Like vultures round a lion slain -
Do you marvel that they won?

Capt. James M. McCann

Notes and Sources

To use the "Notes and Sources" keep in mind these few instructions. At the end of each story is a set of numbers, such as 15/126. The first figure is the "Source," (see list below), and the second is the page number. In a few cases, there are three numbers. The second number indicates the "volume," as found in the *Confederate Veteran* magazine, etc. Example: 1/6/45, means the story came from the *Southern Bivouac*, Volume 6, Page 45.

Notes to the Introduction

1. Beale, 210.
2. Corbin, 51.
3. Andrews, 149.
4. Stiles, 241.
5. Fulton, 48.
6. Smith, 65 & 226.
7. Blackford, 146.
8. Goodloe, 144.
9. Confederate Veteran, (CV), Vol. 3, 134, 270.
10. CV, Vol. 5, 551.
11. CV, Vol. 22, 306.
12. CV, Vol. 2, 90.
13. Figg, 177.
14. Smith, 241, 259.
15. Casler, 103.
16. Johnston, 188.
17. Stiles, 259.
18. Dickert, 200, 395.
19. CV, Vol. 4, 135.
20. Dickert, 168, 290.
21. Bates, 1082.
22. Blackford, 76.
23. CV, Vol. 1, 216.
24. Scribner's, Vol. 17, 33.
25. Polley, "Texas Brigade," 210.
26. McMurray, 124.
27. Casler, 94.
28. Andrews, 81.
29. Stevens, 35.
30. Watkins, 58, 125.
31. Owen, 63.
32. CV, Vol. 6, 512.
33. CV, Vol. 20, 514.
34. CV, Vol. 22, 448.
35. CV, Vol. 23, 124.
36. CV, Vol. 2, 207.
37. Oates, 376.
38. Smith, 187.
39. Figg, 175.
40. Fremantle, 185.
41. Moore, 245.
42. Stevens, 109.
43. Andrews, 123.
44. CV, Vol. 3, 134.
45. McKim, 190.
46. Figg, 27.
47. Johnston, 169.
48. Dickert, 286.
49. CV, Vol. 3, 134.
50. Casler, 164.
51. Smith, 76.
52. Figg, 213.
53. Fremantle, 194.
54. Polley, "Letters," 195.
55. Morgan, 177.
56. Carter, 101.
57. Casler, 164.
58. Musgrove, 221.
59. Dame, 102.
60. Cave, 65.
   Opie, 54.
61. Opie, 55.
62. Robson, 41.
63. Sorrel, 210.
64. Fletcher, 82.
65. Andrews, 90.
   CV, Vol. 3, 220.
66. Musgrove, 195.
   Owen, 128.
   CV, Vol. 6, 432.
67. Smith, 58.
   CV, Vol. 7, 366.
68. CV, Vol. 8, 500.
69. Carter, 53.
   CV, Vol. 6, 268.
70. Andrews, 124.
71. Johnston, 103.
72. Clark, 5.

Sources and Bibliography

1. *The Southern Bivouac.* "The Skirmish Line." Louisville, KY: Vol. II, No. 10. June 1884 and Vol. I, No. 1, June 1885.
2. *Confederate Veteran Magazine.* Nashville, TN: 1893-1932.
3. Dunlop, W.S. *Lee's Sharpshooters.* Little Rock, AR: 1899.
4. Hankins, Samuel W. *The Simple Story of a Soldier.* Nashville, TN: 1912.

5. Bernard, George. Unpublished memoir in the files of the GNMP library.
6. Polley, Joseph B. *Hood's Texas Brigade*. Dayton, OH: 1976.
7. Mosgrove, George D. *Kentucky Cavaliers in Dixie*. Wilmington, NC: 1991.
8. Moore, Edward A. *The Story of a Cannoneer Under Stonewall Jackson*. New York, NY: 1907.
9. Wood, William N. *Reminiscences of Big I*. Jackson, TN: 1956.
10. Morgan, William H. *Personal Reminiscences of the War of 1861-1865*. Freeport, NY: 1971.
11. Stewart, William H. *A Pair of Blankets*. Wilmington, NC: 1990.
12. Howard, James M. *Recollections of a Maryland Confederate Soldier and Staff Officer*. Dayton, OH: 1975.
13. Gordon, John B. *Reminiscences of the Civil War*. New York, NY: 1903.
14. Nisbet, James C. *Four Years on the Firing Line*. Wilmington, NC: 1987.
15. McKim, Randolph H. *A Soldier's Recollections*. Washington, DC: 1983.
16. Dargan, James F. *My Experiences in Service; or a Nine Months Man*. Los Angeles, CA: 1974.
17. Walton, William M. *An Epitome of My Life*. Austin, TX: 1965.
18. Neese, George M. *Three Years in the Confederate Horse Artillery*. Dayton, OH: 1988.
19. Poague, William. *Gunner With Stonewall*. Jackson, TN: 1957.
20. Polley, Joseph B. *A Soldier's Letters To Charming Nellie*. New York, NY: 1908.
21. McCarthy, Carlton. *Detailed Minutiae of Soldier Life in the Army of Northern Virginia. 1861-1865*. Richmond, VA: 1882.
22. Robson, John S. *How a One-Legged Rebel Lives*. Gaithersburg, MD: 1984.
23. Johnston, David E. *The Story of a Confederate Boy in the Civil War*. Radford, VA: 1980.
24. Figg, Royal W. *Where Men Only Dare To Go*. Richmond, VA: 1885.
25. Opie, John N. *A Rebel Cavalryman with Lee, Stuart and Jackson*. Chicago, IL: 1899.
26. Blackford, Wm. W. *War Years with Jeb Stuart*. New York, NY: 1945.
27. Owen, William M. *In Camp and Battle with the Washington Artillery*. Boston, MA: 1885.
28. Green, John W., A. D. Kirwan, Ed. *Johnny Green of the Orphan Brigade*. Lexington, KY: 1956.
29. Smith, William A. *The Anson Guards*. Charlotte, NC: 1914.
30. Myers, Frank M. *The Comanches: A History of White's Battalion, Virginia Cavalry*. Baltimore, MD: 1871.
31. Casler, John O., J. I. Robertson, Jr., Ed. *Four Years in the Stonewall Brigade*. Dayton, OH: 1971.
32. Wilson, LeGrand J. *The Confederate Soldier*. Memphis, TN: 1973.
33. Douglas, Henry K. *I Rode With Stonewall*. Chapel Hill, NC: 1968.
34. Stevens, Jno. W. *Reminiscences of the Civil War*. Hillsboro, TX: 1902.
35. Stevenson, William G. *Thirteen Months in the Rebel Army*. New York, NY: 1959.
36. Dame, William M. *From the Rapidan to Richmond*. Richmond, VA: 1987.
37. Fulton, William F., II. *The War Reminiscences of William F. Fulton, II*. Gaithersburg, MD: 1986.
38. Stiles, Robert. *Four Years Under Marse Robert*. New York, NY: 1903.
39. Clark, Walter A. *Under the Stars and Bars*. Jonesboro, GA: 1987.
40. Cooke, John E. *Wearing of the Gray*. Bloomington, IN: 1977.
41. Carter, Howell. *A Cavalryman's Reminiscences of the Civil War*. New Orleans, LA: 1979.
42. Worsham, John H. *One of Jackson's Foot Cavalry*. New York, NY: 1912.

43. Fletcher, William A. *Rebel Private, Front and Rear.* Washington, DC: 1954.
44. Booth, George W. *Personal Reminiscences of a Maryland Soldier in the War Between the States.* Baltimore, MD: 1898.
45. Watkins, Sam R. *Co. Aytch.* Jackson, TN: 1952.
46. Andrews, William H. *Footprints of a Regiment.* Atlanta, GA: 1992.
47. Cole, Robert T., J. D. Stocker, Ed. *From Huntsville to Appomattox.* Knoxville, TN: 1996.
48. Oates, William C. *The War Between The Union And The Confederacy.* Dayton, OH: 1974.
49. Collins, Robert M. *Chapters From The Unwritten History of the War Between the States.* Dayton, OH: 1988.
50. Mills, George H. *History of the 16th North Carolina Regiment in the Civil War.* Hamilton, NY: 1992.
51. Lamar Rifles. *A History of Company G, Eleventh Mississippi Regiment, C.S.A.* Roanoke, VA: 1903.
52. Grisamore, Silas T., A. W. Bergeron, Jr., Ed. *Reminiscences of Uncle Silas.* Baton Rouge, LA: 1981.
53. Stephenson, Philip D., N. C. Hughes, Jr., Ed. *The Civil War Memoir of Philip D. Stephenson.* Conway, AZ: 1995.
54. Dickert, D. Augustus. *History of Kershaw's Brigade.* Dayton, OH: 1973.
55. Holt, David, T. D. Cockrell and M. B. Ballard, Eds. *A Mississippi Rebel in the Army of Northern Virginia.* Baton Rouge, LA: 1995.
56. *Scribner's Monthly, An Illustrated Magazine.* Vol. XVII, No. 1, New York, NY: 1879.

Greg Coco speaking with servicemen in the Gettysburg National Military Park Soldiers' National Cemetery on July 19, 2005 *(Katie Lawhon, NPS)*.

About the Author

Gregory Ashton Coco, born and raised in Louisiana, lived in the Gettysburg area for nearly 35 years.

In 1972, after serving in the U.S. Army, he earned a degree in American History from the University of Southwestern Louisiana. While in the military, Greg spent a tour of duty in Vietnam as a prisoner of war military interrogator and infantry platoon radio operator with the 25th Infantry and received, among other awards, the Purple Heart and Bronze Star.

During his years in Gettysburg, Greg worked as a National Park Service Ranger and a Licensed Battlefield Guide. He wrote sixteen books and a dozen scholarly articles on Gettysburg and the Civil War. His book *A Strange and Blighted Land. Gettysburg: The Aftermath of a Battle* was voted #12 in the Top 50 Civil War Books ever written.

Greg died at age 62 in February of 2009. In his words, he was "the happy husband of Cindy L. Small for 26 years. He was the fortunate father of daughter Keri E. Coco. He loved them both with all his heart." Keri is married to Cail MacLean and they have a daughter, Ashton MacLean Coco.

.